Albert Camus: A Very Short Introduction

VERY SHORT INTRODUCTIONS are for anyone wanting a stimulating and accessible way into a new subject. They are written by experts, and have been translated into more than 45 different languages.

The series began in 1995, and now covers a wide variety of topics in every discipline. The VSI library currently contains over 600 volumes—a Very Short Introduction to everything from Psychology and Philosophy of Science to American History and Relativity—and continues to grow in every subject area.

## Very Short Introductions available now:

ABOLITIONISM Richard S. Newman
THE ABRAHAMIC RELIGIONS
    Charles L. Cohen
ACCOUNTING Christopher Nobes
ADAM SMITH Christopher J. Berry
ADOLESCENCE Peter K. Smith
ADVERTISING Winston Fletcher
AESTHETICS Bence Nanay
AFRICAN AMERICAN RELIGION
    Eddie S. Glaude Jr
AFRICAN HISTORY John Parker and
    Richard Rathbone
AFRICAN POLITICS Ian Taylor
AFRICAN RELIGIONS
    Jacob K. Olupona
AGEING Nancy A. Pachana
AGNOSTICISM Robin Le Poidevin
AGRICULTURE Paul Brassley and
    Richard Soffe
ALBERT CAMUS Oliver Gloag
ALEXANDER THE GREAT
    Hugh Bowden
ALGEBRA Peter M. Higgins
AMERICAN CULTURAL HISTORY
    Eric Avila
AMERICAN FOREIGN RELATIONS
    Andrew Preston
AMERICAN HISTORY Paul S. Boyer
AMERICAN IMMIGRATION
    David A. Gerber
AMERICAN LEGAL HISTORY
    G. Edward White
AMERICAN NAVAL HISTORY
    Craig L. Symonds

AMERICAN POLITICAL HISTORY
    Donald Critchlow
AMERICAN POLITICAL PARTIES
    AND ELECTIONS L. Sandy Maisel
AMERICAN POLITICS
    Richard M. Valelly
THE AMERICAN PRESIDENCY
    Charles O. Jones
THE AMERICAN REVOLUTION
    Robert J. Allison
AMERICAN SLAVERY
    Heather Andrea Williams
THE AMERICAN WEST Stephen Aron
AMERICAN WOMEN'S HISTORY
    Susan Ware
ANAESTHESIA Aidan O'Donnell
ANALYTIC PHILOSOPHY
    Michael Beaney
ANARCHISM Colin Ward
ANCIENT ASSYRIA Karen Radner
ANCIENT EGYPT Ian Shaw
ANCIENT EGYPTIAN ART AND
    ARCHITECTURE Christina Riggs
ANCIENT GREECE Paul Cartledge
THE ANCIENT NEAR EAST
    Amanda H. Podany
ANCIENT PHILOSOPHY Julia Annas
ANCIENT WARFARE
    Harry Sidebottom
ANGELS David Albert Jones
ANGLICANISM Mark Chapman
THE ANGLO-SAXON AGE John Blair
ANIMAL BEHAVIOUR
    Tristram D. Wyatt

Available soon:

For more information visit our website

www.oup.com/vsi/

Oliver Gloag

# ALBERT CAMUS

## A Very Short Introduction

OXFORD
UNIVERSITY PRESS

# OXFORD
### UNIVERSITY PRESS

Great Clarendon Street, Oxford, OX2 6DP,
United Kingdom

Oxford University Press is a department of the University of Oxford.
It furthers the University's objective of excellence in research, scholarship,
and education by publishing worldwide. Oxford is a registered trade mark of
Oxford University Press in the UK and in certain other countries

© Oliver Gloag 2020

The moral rights of the author have been asserted

First edition published in 2020

Impression: 1

Published in the United States of America by Oxford University Press
198 Madison Avenue, New York, NY 10016, United States of America

British Library Cataloguing in Publication Data
Data available

Library of Congress Control Number: 2019951497

ISBN 978-0-19-879297-0

Printed in Great Britain by
Ashford Colour Press Ltd, Gosport, Hampshire

*For Tracy*

# Contents

# Acknowledgements

This book owes much to the support and counsel of Fredric Jameson. I also owe a debt of gratitude to Frédéric Érard who, along with Ezra Suleiman, helped make space during a tumultuous time. I would also like to thank Fabien le Dantec, Sarah Samadi, Darin Waters, Juan Sánchez-Martinez, John Crutchfield, and Matt Eshleman.

A book depends on the varied perspective of many other commentators, and I would like to acknowledge the joint influence of many previous writers on Camus and in particular, Ian Birchall, Alice Kaplan, Conor Cruise O'Brien, and Edward Said.

My students in Western North Carolina emulate some of the best in Camus's *parcours* in their tireless pursuit of education; they are an inspiration.

Carole Aciman and Pascale Casanova died too soon; they both helped me in different ways with my work on Camus, I am grateful for having known them.

Finally, I would like to thank my wife Tracy Hayes; without her help and support, this book would not have been written.

# List of illustrations

# Preface: Which Camus?

Today, Albert Camus is one of the best-known French philosophers—though he did not consider himself to be one—and perhaps the most read French novelist in the world. His works have inspired numerous movies, even pop music, and heads of state from France and the United States of America have often invoked them favourably.

But which Camus is being celebrated? Is it the fearless reporter who tirelessly investigated the terrible conditions of the people indigenous to the Algerian region of Kabylia occupied by France in the 1930s? Or the man who wrote that the only salvation for France was to remain an 'Arab power'? Do we celebrate the writer who published articles in a clandestine resistance newspaper during the German occupation of France? Surely not the ambitious author who agreed to withdraw his chapter on Kafka to ensure that his philosophical treatise would pass the Nazi-controlled censorship? Is our praise reserved for the author who takes to task marriage, mourning, and social mobility in his most famous novel, *The Stranger*, or the one who, in that same work, does not name any of the Arab characters? When we speak of Camus, do we mean the resister who was in favour of the death penalty, or the philosopher who later condemned it?

Camus was profoundly conflicted. He was a firm believer in the egalitarian ideals of French enlightenment in part because the French state effectively supported him after the loss of his father during the First World War and provided him with the means, through education, to lift himself out of the resulting poverty of his youth. However, the hardships he experienced at that time, and his upbringing in French-colonized Algeria, made him increasingly aware of how France's oppression of Arabs and Berbers contradicted these egalitarian ideals. Throughout his life and works, Camus oscillated between avoiding this contradiction and confronting it. Ultimately, this duality became his identity. The conflicting impulses toward repressing and coming to terms with this awareness drove his writing in different ways at different times.

This short book will provide the reader with an overview of Camus's life and works and will also squarely address the ambiguities of Camus's positions because they are integral to understanding both his major works and his renewed popularity today.

# Chapter 1
# Camus, son of France in Algeria

All too often Camus's works (particularly *The Stranger*) have been considered only as free-standing masterpieces of French literature. However, questions of identity and historical context become more pronounced in the colonial situation. To grasp fully and appreciate Camus's achievements and the ambiguity of his works, it is important to consider the historical situation that shaped his formative years.

Albert Camus (1913–60) was a French citizen born in Algeria. He would live there from his birth until the middle of the Second World War. His father, Lucien Camus, worked as a foreman in a vineyard in the district of Mondovi, about 100 miles east of Algiers. Lucien married Catherine Hélène Sintès, a homemaker, on 13 November 1910, and three months later, Albert's older brother—also named Lucien—was born. Albert was born in Mondovi nearly three years later, on 7 November 1913.

The ancestry of Camus's family is closely tied to France's presence in Algeria. Records indicate that his paternal great-grandfather, Claude Camus, came to Algeria in 1834, shortly after France's conquest. His maternal grandfather, Étienne Sintès, was born in Algiers in 1850, though Étienne's wife, Catherine Marie Cardona, was born in Spain. Camus's lineage was typical of French citizens born and living in Algeria, who were called *pieds-noirs*, literally, 'black feet'. In the early 20th century, *pieds-noirs* originally referred to the mostly Arab shipmen who worked barefoot in the charcoal bunker in the hull of the ship. During the Algerian War of Independence (1954–62), the term eventually denoted all French citizens born and living in Algeria. (This is how I will refer to the French settlers throughout this book.)

At the time of Camus's birth, on the eve of the First World War, Algeria was officially a French region divided into three *départements* (Oran, Alger, and Constantine) and three military zones, all under the authority of a governor-general. In reality, however, there were two Algerias. One was a French region, inhabited by 750,000 *pieds-noirs* who had all the rights and protections afforded by the French Republic. They were French citizens, equal under one legal system—they had the right to vote and lived under the famous French revolutionary slogan: *liberté, égalité, fraternité*. In the other Algeria, an occupied territory, there were 4.7 million 'Muslims' as the French census called them. These men and women were not French citizens (though they had the obligations of French nationals) and they lived under a set of punitive laws that made it difficult for them to receive an education, to earn a living, to speak their language, to practise their religion, or to own land. (For the purposes of this book, I will call them Algerians (which includes Arabs and Berbers), but the French authorities referred to them most often as *indigènes* or Muslims.)

The history of France's involvement with Algeria was nearly 100 years old by the time of Camus's birth. Algeria was invaded in 1830 by the army of King Charles X, initially as an attempt to create a diversion from domestic challenges to the legitimacy of his regime. After the invasion, France's presence gradually grew. Until 1870, Algeria was under the control of the French military, governed by a succession of generals. The conquest of Algeria by France was long and drawn out, with some historians estimating that over 6 million Algerians died over the nearly 100 years of occupation.

During the conquest, the French took millions of acres of land from Algerians, uprooting entire crops. (Typically, they replaced olive trees with vines to produce wine for France.) During this period, in pursuit of territorial control, they routinely resorted to razing entire villages and killing many inhabitants (a practice called *la razzia*) and forcing enemy combatants into caves, the entrances of which they then set on fire, asphyxiating the prisoners inside (*l'enfumade*). These actions were officially sanctioned by the authorities and praised by prominent intellectuals at the time, including Alexis de Tocqueville, who wrote in a report on Algeria: 'I believe that the laws of war allow us to ravage the country and that this must be done either by destroying harvests...or by way of these rapid incursions we call *razzias*...'.

As a result, there were many uprisings and revolts against French rule, the largest of which lasted over six years and was led by Abdel El Kader, who defeated Governor-General Thomas-Robert Bugeaud, before eventually becoming a prisoner of the French in 1847. By 1871, the last of the major Algerian insurrections failed. French civilian governments ruled Algeria for the next eighty-three years, until the first year of the Algerian War of Independence in 1954.

As a child Camus may not have known the true history of France's conquest and occupation of Algeria. The French educational system put forth an alternative set of 'official' facts; 'it was the indigenous people themselves who provoked France's attacks on them' is a standard line from French history books in the 1920s, which consistently praised 'France's magnificent colonial empire' and omitted any mention of the *razzias*, *enfumades*, or land confiscations. This lack of acknowledgement continued for many years and France only officially recognized the Algerian War of Independence in 2002.

What young Camus could not ignore and would come to challenge in his mid-twenties was the second-class status of Algerians.

3

After the last insurrection was quelled in 1871 and after the fall of Napoleon III, French-occupied Algeria changed drastically. Under the Third Republic, the military policy of working with Arab and Berber tribal leaders was abandoned, and the new civilian leadership exerted direct control over the Arabs and Berbers via the *Code Indigène* (literally, indigenous code). In contrast to the famous *Code Civil* that was and still is the rule of law for French citizens, the *Code Indigène*, which was put in place in 1881 and only partly revoked by President Charles de Gaulle in 1944, set out punitive laws and regulations specifically for Arabs and Berbers. Just like former slaves in the French Caribbean islands, Algerians needed to obtain a permit to travel outside their villages. Muslim religious practices were increasingly under the control of the French state (for example, many koranic schools were shut down and pilgrimage to Mecca was rarely authorized), and specific tribunals for Muslims, judged by Frenchmen, offered virtually no right of appeal. Non-Europeans had to pay a special supplemental 'Arab tax', and Algerians could not vote in any elections.

In the standard playbook of colonial powers, a classic move is to recruit—via the granting of a privileged status—a minority ethnic or religious group to assist in governing the conquered land. France attempted this move with Algerian Jews, though it was far from successful at first. The Jews living in Algeria (called *Israélites indigènes* by the French government) had the same legal status as Arabs and Berbers and were not considered French citizens. In 1869, they were offered French citizenship, but virtually all declined; most of them spoke Arabic and had no more ties to France than other indigenous people of Algeria; they were Arabs: culturally, ethnically, and linguistically.

The French government, faced with this show of indifference by Algerian Jews, which it took as a rejection, unilaterally proclaimed all Algerian Jews French citizens in October 1870. This famous Crémieux decree of mass naturalization unleashed a torrent of anti-Semitism from the *pieds-noirs* towards Algerian Jews. The *pieds-noirs* from virtually all political parties were afraid that the naturalization of Algerian Jews was a harbinger of things to come: in short, that Arabs and Berbers might eventually be naturalized as well, and that their own privileged status in French Algeria would then be threatened.

From 1870 onwards a constant feature of life in French Algeria was virulent and often violent anti-Semitism. There were many 'anti-Jewish leagues', and there was even a very popular anti-Jewish party. Pogroms took place in Oran in 1897, and in Constantine in 1934, which resulted in many deaths and mutilations of Jewish Algerians. When Marshal Pétain came to power in July 1940, the Crémieux decree was revoked: Algerian Jews lost their French citizenship and again shared the same status as Arabs and Berbers until the end of the Second World War.

Subject to constant denigration and sometimes violent attacks by *pieds-noirs*, Algerian Jews were nevertheless legally French from 1870 to 1940. Over time they came to consider themselves as *pieds-noirs* and many sided with France during the Algerian War of Independence.

Though the French state never considered naturalizing all Arabs or Berbers, the judicial segregation of Algerians via the *Code Indigène* was concurrent with a policy of incremental integration. This seemingly contradictory objective of integrating a small minority of Algerians in the school system to create a local elite who would then work within and for the French Republic was highly controversial for the vast majority of *pieds-noirs*. The policy of limited integration meant that Algerians—those very few who could afford the fees for food (and housing if it was a boarding school)—were allowed in public schools, albeit in very small numbers. In Camus's secondary school class, for example, there were only three Arabs out of thirty students.

Some members of the educated Algerian elite made a militant push for more integration. In 1912, a coalition of this elite was organized as a group called 'The Young Algerians', and, led by Benthami Ould Hamida, travelled to Paris to present their 'Young Algerians Manifesto'. The demands outlined in the Manifesto on the whole did not challenge the French presence in Algeria but did include the abolition of the *Code Indigène*. The Manifesto was rejected by the French government, but the movement would strengthen into an organized political force in the 1930s. In 1936 Camus himself supported the abolition of the *Code Indigène* and the granting of citizenship for a small minority of Algerians. He hoped for a time when France's treatment of Algerians would reflect the humanist rhetoric of the French Republic.

When the First World War broke out in Europe in 1914, France summoned Algerians to join the French army. Few were keen to fight for what they saw as occupying forces. In at least one recorded instance, the population of one region (*les Aurès*) rose up against the draft. The uprising was brutally repressed, the region was bombarded, and hundreds of insurgents were killed. Of the sizeable contingent of Algerians who fought under the French flag, a disproportionate number died on the battlefields of Europe, as they were routinely sent to the most dangerous combat zones. Still, many *pieds-noirs* died as well, and Camus's father Lucien was amongst them.

## Camus's three fathers

Lucien Auguste Camus died from his wounds in the early stages of the First World War, when his son Albert was only 1 year old. Camus's mother Catherine, half-deaf and illiterate, was unable to raise her two sons alone. Thus, Camus grew up very modestly in the home of his stern grandmother (Catherine-Maria Sintès), who often beat him and was steadfastly against his pursuing his studies (she was the likely inspiration for the unmourned mother in *The Stranger*). His uncle, a barrel-maker who could barely speak, also lived with them (he was the subject of a short story, *The Silent Men*), along with his mother and Camus's older brother Lucien (see Figure 1). The five members of the Camus-Sintès family lived in a tiny apartment with an outhouse. Camus and his brother Lucien shared a bed in the same room as their mother.

With the loss of his father, until then the sole breadwinner in his family, the young Albert was adopted by the French state, and not just symbolically. With their adoption, Camus and his brother immediately became wards of the state (*pupilles de la nation*), entitling each of them to free medical care for life and a modest allowance. Camus's mother took up cleaning houses and as a war widow she also received a yearly pension of 800 francs, a modest amount compared to the average monthly salary for a *pied-noir*, though it compared favourably to the one franc a day Algerian labourers made working in the fields.

1. In the workshop of Camus's uncle in Algiers in 1920: Albert Camus (7 years old) is in the centre in a black suit.

Camus would have two major mentors in his youth: his primary school teacher Louis Germain, followed by the philosopher and professor Jean Grenier during his secondary school and university years. Each was to play a critical role in Camus's life. As Jules Ferry (1832–93), the founder of the French secular, mandatory, and free school system, often stated, 'teachers are in effect soldiers of the French republic', whose mission was to be the aide and sometimes the replacement for the head of the family.

In Camus's posthumous novel *The First Man*, which was largely autobiographical, there are many references to his relationship with Louis Germain and his role as more than a teacher. Germain took an immediate interest in Camus, coming to his home and giving him private lessons, all free of charge, to help him obtain a scholarship and entry to secondary school (which would otherwise have been prohibitively expensive). Germain was also a stern disciplinarian who often used corporal punishment on his students (including young Albert). When Camus was accepted in secondary school, Germain convinced his grandmother to allow him to attend—even though he would not be working and contributing financially to the household. This young, fatherless boy from the rough *pieds-noirs* neighbourhood was nurtured and encouraged (sometimes harshly), and finally made it to secondary school on a scholarship and then to the university, all because of Germain's support. We can imagine that school, and in particular French literature, a subject in which Camus excelled, became a way out of the dreariness of his environment and the relative poverty of his home.

Camus's gratitude toward Germain was not short-lived: over thirty years later he famously dedicated his Nobel Prize for Literature to his primary school teacher: 'without you, without that supportive hand that you lent to the poor child that I was, without your teaching and your example, I never would have made it.'

When he was 17, Camus passed the first part of his *baccalauréat*. This accomplishment occurred in June 1930, during the celebrations of the centennial of the French presence in Algeria. For the now nearly one million *pieds-noirs*, it was a long party. French authorities organized and funded numerous parades and concerts, unveiled monuments and plaques, and opened museums, all to the glory of France's *mission civilisatrice* ('civilizing mission'). Even the famous left-leaning French director Jean Renoir was commissioned to make an adventure movie glorifying colonizers (*Le Bled*). Few of the six million Arabs and Berbers participated. Did Camus join in the celebrations? Little is known of the specifics of his life at this stage save that, like many 17-year-olds, he loved to play soccer for the local team.

Camus started what should have been his last year of secondary school in the autumn of 1930, but his life changed drastically when one day in December he started coughing blood. The hospital's diagnosis was grim: tuberculosis. Treatment for TB was limited to warmth, rest, and good nutrition, and the disease was a lifelong condition. Many years later, Camus told a friend that on that day in the hospital he was afraid for his life and that the expression on the doctor's face confirmed his fear. His reaction may have also been the result of his staying in a communal room at the Mustapha hospital: a facility where most patients were Arab. According to one biographer, Camus was frightened by the dismal conditions in the hospital and wanted to go home immediately.

From this time on, Camus had a radically new perspective, one in which the arbitrariness and inevitability of death were impossible to ignore. At only 17, Camus became aware of his own mortality. This sudden awareness of death would have many ramifications. In his first philosophical work, *The Myth of Sisyphus*, the acute awareness of mortality is inextricably linked to his theory of the absurd. In his fiction as well, the imminence and randomness of death are central: death wantonly applied in *Caligula*, death as a certainty (but also liberating) in *The Stranger*, death by disease in *The Plague*.

His prolonged absence from school led his philosophy professor Jean Grenier to pay him a visit—an unusual move for a professor. During this visit, which was later memorialized by both Camus and Grenier in their correspondence and in Grenier's memoirs, Camus remained silent and seemingly standoffish, though he would later write that he was simultaneously moved by the gesture and unable to express his feelings. This visit also marked the beginning of a lifelong friendship between the two men. Grenier was perhaps the single most important intellectual influence in Camus's life, and in his early years he acted as a veritable intellectual and political mentor. Camus would dedicate his first book—a collection of essays titled *Betwixt and Between*—to Grenier.

Grenier was not just a professor; he was a freethinker who rejected all orthodoxy or system. He had already published two philosophical essays before he met Camus. Crucially, Grenier also had connections in Paris, where he had worked for the prestigious *Nouvelle Revue française*, a publication which featured the writings of the best authors of what was a veritable golden age of French literature. He knew and had worked with towering literary figures such as André Malraux, André Gide, Henry de Montherlant, and Max Jacob. Grenier's importance in Camus's intellectual life is evident in one of his first diary entries, written when Camus was only 19 years old:

> ...read Grenier's book. He is in it completely and I feel the love and admiration he inspires in me grow....Two hours spent with him always augment me. Will I ever realize all that I owe him?

But in the beginning of 1931, there were more immediate and concrete consequences of TB for young Camus. Doctors recommended he leave the cramped apartment on rue Belcour in

Algiers, which was no place for extended convalescence. Very soon, Camus moved in with his uncle Gustave Arcault, who also lived in Algiers and was married to Antoinette Sintès, Camus's maternal aunt. He would never return home. Arcault was an eccentric character, a butcher with a handlebar mustache who spent a lot of time holding court in the local café. Moreover, Arcault was a voracious reader; the works of Voltaire, Anatole France, and James Joyce lined his bookshelves.

Camus read Arcault's books and lent a hand in the butcher's shop where Arcault attempted to groom him to be his successor. During his time with the childless Arcault couple, Camus's life became one of relative affluence compared to his living standards at his grandmother's home. He had a room of his own, and he ate red meat every day. (Doctor's orders: in the 1930s French physicians believed that meat was a good treatment for TB.) Reminiscing many years later while being interviewed by a friend, Camus considered Arcault as a 'sort of' father figure in his life.

The ongoing threat to Camus's life of TB was also a liberation. At the Arcaults' home Camus plunged into his studies with renewed intensity and guidance and support from Grenier. Camus's outlook had changed as well. He now connected his awareness of death's certainty with freedom, a central paradox that was at the core of his future works.

After six months of convalescence, Camus returned for his last year of secondary school and was later awarded a scholarship to enrol in a rigorous two-year preparatory programme for the French national university examination. Success in this examination typically led to admission to the elite Parisian school the *École Normale Supérieure* (ENS), and almost automatically thereafter to the most prestigious posts in the French educational system. But, after his first year at the preparatory school, Camus gave up the goal of admission to the ENS. The second year of the preparatory programme was not offered anywhere in Algeria, so he would have had to live in Paris, a financial strain. His ailing health was also a major obstacle to such a move.

Undeterred by this new setback, Camus continued to pursue different paths and, inspired by Grenier, he seems to have formed his ambition to become a writer in his own right. He continued his studies in Algiers and registered for the equivalent of a master's degree in literature; however, a year later he would change fields and specialize in philosophy instead. Camus's decision not to pursue the preparatory classes meant that he lost his premium scholarship and had to find a job. Camus always worked to fund his studies. In secondary school he worked in a grocery store during the summers and later at his uncle's butcher's shop, and as a university student he worked as a tutor and spent summers working for the city of Algiers in the office in charge of automobile registrations. Camus disliked this bureaucratic work in particular, which he called mind-numbing. He was perpetually strapped for money, until he married the well-to-do Simone Hié in 1934.

Hié was the talk of Camus's world, known for her risqué dresses and for her promiscuous behaviour. In the very patriarchal Algiers of the 1930s such behaviour was more than scandalous. Camus took an immediate liking to her, but there was one problem: she was the fiancée of one of his good friends, Max-Pol Fouchet, who was often away on militant errands for the socialist party. Upon his return from such a trip, Camus told Max-Pol that Hié was not coming back to him.

When Camus and Hié married in 1934, Camus was 21 and Hié 20. Hié's mother was a successful ophthalmologist, and Simone represented another world in terms of values and class—perhaps this was part of her appeal. Certainly, it was a step up in the world for the son of a cleaning lady to marry the daughter of a wealthy doctor. Once they married, Hié's mother paid for their flat in a nice part of town, close to Jean Grenier. The Arcaults, impressed by the marriage, sent the couple some money and loaned them a car.

From its start, the marriage was tumultuous and featured many breaks and reconciliations. Unlike Camus, Hié failed her *baccalauréat* and appeared to lack purpose or direction. She was also addicted to opiates. As the marriage went on, her addiction became pronounced and she spent more and more time in rehabilitation centres. In 1936, during a trip to Europe, Camus discovered a letter addressed to his wife from a doctor who supplied her with drugs and who also was obviously her lover. For Camus this was the last straw: their short marriage was for all intents and purposes over; upon returning to Algiers, he moved out. The divorce was finalized in February 1940.

Camus continued his studies in Algiers. He was now well on the way to take another national examination: the *agrégation*. Passing this crucial exam would have made him—like Jean Grenier—one of the top secondary school professors, a *fonctionnaire* (employee of the state) with plenty of leisure time to pursue his literary ambitions. For Camus, education and his studies were always essentially just a means to an end: to have time to write. Even his mentor and friend Grenier seemed to have doubts about Camus's dedication to his studies. Later, in an otherwise laudatory book on his most famous student, Grenier would say that he was 'not an avid reader'. Nevertheless, Camus was often influenced by the material he studied at university. For example, one of his classes on Roman emperors probably inspired the subject matter of his first play, *Caligula*, which he began to write around the time he attended the course.

Despite this lack of passion for his studies, in order to sit for the examination Camus had to write a substantial final thesis. It was titled 'Christian and Neoplatonic Metaphysics: Saint Augustine and Plotinus'. Camus's authorized biographer Oliver Todd details how Camus did not give proper attribution to many sources, sometimes even passing off other scholars' work as his own, and concludes nonchalantly that Camus was *'un pompeur'*, French slang for plagiarist. The board (which included Grenier) that read Camus's thesis did not seem to have been bothered by this transgression: Camus got his diploma.

In the spring of 1936, at the age of 22, with diploma in hand, Camus was ready to sit for the *agrégation* and join Grenier among the ranks of elite secondary school professors. This was not to happen.

## Camus the aspiring writer

The earliest written work we have from Camus consists mainly of papers from his last year of secondary school onwards, which Jean Grenier had encouraged him to submit to *Sud* ('South'), the school's publication. Camus's published and unpublished pieces from this time demonstrate a romantic outlook: he praised nature, especially the sun and its light, and rejected progress, which he likened to a prison. In a piece on music, he stated that great music and great art could not—should not—be understood.

Already at this early stage his ambivalence toward scholarly, academic knowledge is clear. In one of his early unpublished texts, he imagined a dialogue between a first-person narrator and a madman in which he wrote, 'refusing to know is a liberation, a definitive step toward the emancipation of the soul'. This glorification of the acceptance of the unknowable announced some aspects of the absurd which he would develop in *The Myth of Sisyphus*. In another passage from the same unpublished text, the narrator is looking at passers by from his balcony, when the madman admonishes him to disregard these unexamined lives. A much later passage of *The Stranger* epitomizes this attitude— looking down from a balcony at people predictably going about their lives. These passages, and many others, show that Camus at an early age already felt isolated from people who lived their lives without awareness.

The writing from this period is also quite lyrical. As he searched for a voice as a writer, he tried out many genres: poetry, essays—even a fairy tale. At this early stage in his life, if he were to be compared to a painter, perhaps Camus's outlook most resembled some of J. M. W. Turner's more abstract paintings, where the sun's light overwhelms all else and human beings are comparatively insignificant. Camus's religion in those days was Art (which he almost always capitalized), and his perspective was very much influenced by proponents of 'art for art's sake'. He particularly idolized the 19th-century poet Charles Baudelaire—in fact, there are records of Camus and his friends reciting one of Baudelaire's poems, 'The Stranger'. The importance of this poem for Camus is self-evident, because it shares the title and some of the themes of what will become his most famous novel:

—Whom do you love the best, enigmatic man? Tell me. Your father, your
    mother, your sister or your brother?
—I have neither father nor mother, nor sister, nor brother.
—Your friends?
—You use a word there whose meaning leaves me clueless to this day.
—Your country then?
—I don't even know which latitude it resides in.
—Beauty?
—Beauty? I would love her willingly, were she a goddess and immortal.
—Gold?
—I hate it as much as you hate God.
—Well! What do you love, extraordinary stranger?
—I love the clouds…the clouds that pass…up there…up there…the
    marvellous clouds!

Camus also imitated Baudelaire's dandyism in dress: he wore bow ties, double-breasted suits, felt hats, and white socks (see Figure 2). This attire gave absolutely no indication of his modest origins, but his writing, although not overtly autobiographical, certainly did. He wrote about his family members, his neighbourhood, and

2. **Albert Camus as a young dandy in Florence.**

his own life including his experience in the crowded hospital room on the day he was diagnosed with TB. In *Betwixt and Between* Camus described his life in the small apartment on rue Belcour. The second essay, titled 'Irony', describes his family:

> All five lived together: the grandmother, her middle son, her older daughter, and the two children of that last one. The son was almost mute, the daughter was disabled and it was difficult for her to think. Of her two children, one already worked for an insurance company, when the youngest one pursued his studies.

As in his life, the grandmother dies and his daughter's youngest son (a stand-in for Camus) feels absolutely no grief. Only the beauty of the sun and of the sky provoke authentic and uplifting emotions in the essay.

In this and other writings, the harshness of daily life and the certainty of death become major themes. But the power and potency of moments of communion with nature remain. Many of his essays juxtapose these seeming opposites: the meaninglessness of a life destined for death and moments of elevated happiness, perhaps even bliss, caused by nature. Camus would famously give these moments of bliss a name: '*bonheur*'. *Bonheur* is more forceful than its English equivalent of happiness. There is nothing stronger and more positive than those moments of *bonheur* in Camus's works: they are the ultimate goal, short-lived but repeatable solace from a resolutely hostile human environment and a meaningless world.

## Young Camus and politics

At first it might seem that Camus was apolitical. In his early texts he professed to be against progress and certainly seemed to prefer the writers focused on *l'art pour l'art* to the *artistes engagés*, socially and politically committed artists such as those taught in the French schools: Voltaire and Zola. (There is speculation among some Camus specialists that in his secondary school he might have worked as an editor of a small radical pro-independence paper, *Ikdam*, but no concrete evidence supports this proposition.) There is no record of his being friends or having meaningful interactions with the few Algerian students in secondary school, although he was aware of the Algerians' plight. Years later, when writing to Grenier about his impoverished youth, he relativized his condition, 'I was poor, but would have been worse off had I been Arab.'

Seemingly unexpectedly, however, in the autumn of 1935 at the age of 21 Camus joined the Communist Party and was given the task of recruiting Algerian members. There are several possible explanations for this political commitment, which does not seem to follow from his early writings, and which also appears to contradict his later pronouncements against communism and the Soviet Union. Though not a member himself, Grenier encouraged Camus to join the party. The fact that the Communist Party was the place to be for an aspiring intellectual in the 1930s must have influenced Grenier's recommendation. Many of the greatest names in French literature were either party sympathizers or members, and two of the writers that Camus most admired at the time, Gide and Malraux, were fellow travellers when Camus joined.

But Camus was not a Marxist. Nor was he remotely interested in reading Marx. Camus joined the party in part because it was a place where he could advocate a compromise solution to the growing unrest in certain sectors of the Algerian population. He wanted to promote a gradual integration of Algerians as citizens of the French Republic, was in favour of the abolition of the *Code Indigène*, and supported the granting of citizenship to a minority of Algerians selected from the elites. This compromise would be a way to counter growing unrest from Algerian political groups vocally demanding independence. The proposal of citizenship for a limited number of Algerians formed the basis of the proposed Blum–Viollette bill, named after French prime minister Léon Blum and the bill's main sponsor, Maurice Viollette, a former governor of Algeria.

Camus supported the bill enthusiastically. He wrote a petition, 'Manifesto of Intellectuals in Favour of the Viollette Bill', in which he urged for a repeal of the *Code Indigène*, which he called inhuman. Camus also wrote that the bill was in the national interest as it showed the Arab people France's human face, something that he stated must be done. Thus Camus supported a strategic but problematic position: colonialism with a human face—whose ultimate objective was to safeguard France's presence in Algeria.

Camus was rightly convinced that refusing to make concessions to the Arab people would have dire consequences for France as a colonial power. This was also Viollette's position. He issued a stern warning to the *pieds-noirs* that the lack of a compromise would strengthen the credibility of Algerians in favour of a complete break with France and independence. But the warning went unheeded. Faced with resounding opposition from *pieds-noirs*, the bill never made it into law and was rejected in the autumn of 1937. The Communist Party also abandoned support of a compromise bill, which led the party to lose some of its Arab members and left Camus demoralized. Whether he left the party or was excluded from it is still a matter of debate, but after the failure of the Blum–Viollette bill, it is clear that Camus had no desire to remain a member.

Camus's sojourn in the Communist Party permanently influenced his life and artistic endeavours, albeit not in the way the party would have wanted. In what was perhaps the most important legacy of his years as a member, Camus co-founded a theatrical troupe called Theatre of Labour. He co-wrote a militant play about an insurrectional miners' strike in the region of Asturias in Spain right before the Spanish Civil War (*Revolt in Asturias*). Although the play supported the insurrectional workers, a striking ambiguity in Camus's political beliefs began to emerge. The passages that Camus is said to have written (according to the standard French edition) include strong criticism of the violence caused both by the Spanish state and by the miners and their party. In the eyes of Camus, revolutionary violence was just as unacceptable as state violence. For a play written about events on the eve of the Spanish Civil War, which would lead to an upsurge of artistic and intellectual support for the Spanish republicans who fought and lost against Franco, this was a strange position to take. The problem of revolutionary violence was to become a constant in Camus's works and would emerge in his later debates with Sartre and in his play *The Just Assassins*.

Camus's short time as a member of the Communist Party was the first outward manifestation of his acute—but until then hidden—awareness of the injustices of French colonialism. Certainly, by joining the Communist Party, Camus shifted abruptly from a position of silence on colonial realities to a decision to confront them. Yet Camus's stance was one of compromise: he wanted to reform, to modify colonialism, but he never challenged France's authority over Algerian land nor was he ever in favour of Algerian independence. His first experience of revolutionary and parliamentary politics made him realize that his goal of a better integration of Algerians to the French colonial system in the face of staunch opposition by the vast majority of *pieds-noirs* was well-nigh impossible. Camus would later express displeasure when critics mentioned his membership of the Communist Party—not only because he became extremely critical of the Communist Party and of the USSR, but perhaps also because his time as a political militant provided a bleak reminder of the intractable chasm between Algerians and *pieds-noirs*.

Around the time Camus left the party, he focused on theatre as a playwright and actor. While a member of the Theatre of Labour, Camus had many girlfriends but his real love was Francine Faure, a brilliant student of mathematics and music who did not immediately reciprocate his advances. He courted her assiduously and she would eventually become his second wife.

To make ends meet, he found employment as a clerk with the meteorological institute in Algiers. His literary projects were many: he worked on a play (*Caligula*), a novel (*The Happy Death*, published posthumously), and a series of essays (*Nuptials*) and attempted to launch a literary journal with friends (two issues were published). But, in October 1938, another setback would change the course of his life. Following a compulsory medical check-up on 8 October, the French educational system barred him by law from joining the French civil service because of his poor health. (To preserve state resources, citizens with a short life expectancy could not become government functionaries.) Camus appealed the decision to no avail. He must have felt that all his work from primary school to university was, on some level, meaningless. He would not follow in the footsteps of Grenier after all.

Almost immediately after he learned of his rejection, a crucial encounter would alter his course yet again. That same October, Camus met Pascal Pia, an ambitious journalist from Paris who was tasked with starting *Alger républicain*, a left-leaning daily newspaper in Algiers. Pia and Camus had a lot in common. Both had lost their fathers at war and were raised by their mothers, and both were admirers of Baudelaire. Pia wanted Camus to be an associate editor and reporter at his paper. Camus, though ambivalent, accepted. (In a letter to Grenier Camus confessed that had he not been rejected by the French civil service, he would not have joined Pia.)

Despite his apparent reluctance, Camus quickly embraced his new position; he worked everywhere on the newspaper: in the printing room, as a copy editor, in the courts, and most famously as an investigative reporter and editorialist. Camus's involvement with journalism would last the rest of his life. It would lead him to challenge the authorities in many (over 150) articles, and eventually to the editorship of France's most prestigious resistance paper. However, in 1938, on the eve of the Second World War, Camus was embarking on a career as a bona fide muckraker. His most frequent target? The French colonial administration.

# Chapter 2
# Camus, from reporter to editorialist

Camus became a journalist during the tumultuous 1930s. Hitler was in power in Germany. The Spanish Civil War had been raging for two years and would end in 1939 with the victory of the military dictatorship led by Franco. Meanwhile, in France, a coalition of a different kind had taken over: the joining together of all the parties of the left led to the first French Jewish head of government, Léon Blum. Following his ascendance, workers occupied factories throughout France, an action which spurred the newly elected government to enact numerous progressive social reforms including a reduced working week and guaranteed paid vacations. These changes dramatically improved the quality of life for most mainland French citizens. This movement, its government, and its policies were all known as the Popular Front.

In this context, Camus continued his own kind of commitment to social justice as a journalist in Pascal Pia's *Alger républicain*. It was a small paper, with a small staff. Camus was in charge of the judicial beat—an experience he would put to good use in *The Stranger*. Pia, not only editor-in-chief and a left-wing journalist, was a man of letters as well as a supporter of the Popular Front. The masthead of *Alger républicain* was subtitled 'journal des travailleurs', the workers' paper. Although its editorials supported the advocates of democracy in the Spanish Civil War, it would be a proponent of appeasement with Hitler's Germany.

One of Camus's first opinion pieces, a short editorial written in October 1938, was very much in the spirit of the Popular Front, with the interests of French workers in mind—but some workers more than others. Camus's central point was that pay increases resulting from the Popular Front strikes were negated by cost of living increases. He concluded with a call for salaries to be indexed to the cost of living. However, he mentions but does not challenge the fact that in Algeria, there was a two-tiered system, and *pieds-noirs* workers' salaries went from 6 to 7.20 francs per hour while Algerian workers' salaries went from 1.40 to 2.30 per hour. He cited these figures not to criticize the disparity between indigenous and European workers, but rather to decry the fact that the rise for the *pieds-noirs* workers was insignificant compared to the almost doubled salary increase for their Algerian counterparts. Camus based his reasoning on the colonial hierarchy: he took for granted the fact that the salaries of *pieds-noirs* were still three times as high as the salaries of Algerians. This early editorial captures Camus's ambiguous political position: he wanted justice for all, but only within the confines of an unjust colonial society.

Camus's ambivalence about the colonial order comes to the forefront in another article titled 'These men we have erased from humanity', in which he describes his visit to a prison-ship that transported 609 detainees. On one level his article is a straightforward denunciation of the living conditions inside the ship: the quarters are extremely cramped, there are four small cages, each housing 100 prisoners; there is almost no lighting. Camus writes, ill at ease: 'I am not very proud to be here.' Yet, when one of these prisoners asks him for a cigarette, which Camus interprets as a plea for a gesture of complicity and of humanity, he is in a bind: quoting the rules would be futile, so he decides to ignore him. This slow-motion expression of Camus's torment facing the plight of a prisoner is telling: although Camus empathizes, he ignores his request. He feels sympathy for the oppressed, but ultimately he will not break the rules. This dilemma, writ large, is what Camus faced with colonialism.

Camus continues to think of the man who asked him for a cigarette. Camus does not really take a stand on these prisoners of the French state; he speculates that the true horror of their plight is that they have no recourse. Behind his statement of neutrality, he wishes those criminals could appeal their sentences. Here again his reformism is present in veiled form. He doesn't want to contest the judicial system; he wants to reform it and to create more protections for the disenfranchised. He wants to make the colonial system more humane.

Another short piece titled 'Unfortunate Arrests' was emblematic of Camus's position on the rights of Algerians. On 14 July 1939, France's Bastille Day, thousands of militants for independence belonging to Messali Hadj's Party for the People of Algeria demonstrated against colonial rule. Three demonstrators and four party leaders were detained and then provisionally released. The French Popular Front government had banned Hadj's previous party, the North African Star. Now militants of his new party were being harassed, beaten, and jailed by the French authorities. The treatment incensed Camus. Why? Because, in his words, 'actions like these...are as harmful for the prestige of France as for its future'.

Camus then called for the release of the three demonstrators, a courageous stance in 1939 French Algeria. Yet Camus's concluding sentence in the editorial showed that his objective was not as controversial as it might initially have seemed: '...the only way to *eliminate* Algerian nationalism is to suppress the injustice it is born out of.' This statement was at the heart of Camus's position on Algeria: he wanted to eliminate Algerian nationalism and thought that adopting a conciliatory approach was the best means to that end. Camus rightly sensed that France's intransigence towards Algerians would be its undoing. Thus, he proposed the release of the prisoners and broadly advocated more social rights and a better life for Algerians—but only under French rule.

In short, Camus was in favour of assimilation; he wanted to find the best way for Algerians to remain French, and for France to remain in Algeria. This stance was at the heart of his most famous series of articles written about the region of Kabylia.

## Reportage in Kabylia

Kabylia is a mountainous region of Algeria populated by the Kabyle people, a Berber ethnic group. The Kabyle people were some of the fiercest resisters to France's invasion. As early as 1830 they fought against the Gallic invaders and not until 1857 did the French assume power in the region, albeit precariously. A majority of the founding members of Hadj's pro-independence party were Kabyle. France's response was neglect—an approach Camus strongly disagreed with, on humanitarian and strategic grounds.

Camus wrote a series of eleven articles which included his impressions of visits to the small villages of the mountains of Kabylia and his conversations with locals, interspersed with facts and figures relating to schooling, life expectancy, and so on. In the articles, known collectively as 'The misery of Kabylia', Camus described lack of running water and sewerage, the poor condition of the homes, and most of all the lack of doctors. Almost two decades later, in 1958 in the middle of the Algerian War of Independence, Camus reprinted seven of the original eleven articles in an attempt to demonstrate his continued concern for Algerians and in particular for Kabyles.

However, the four articles which he chose not to reprint contain some of the most telling passages. In the first article, 'Greece in Rags', Camus described his reaction upon witnessing the utter desolation of the Kabyle people:

> I cannot forget this inhabitant of the indigenous city, Bordj-
> Menaiel, who showed me the body of his little girl, extremely skinny

and in rags and who told me: 'don't you think that this little girl, if I clothed her, if I could keep her clean and feed her, don't you think she would be as beautiful as any French girl?' And how could I forget [him] since *I had such a guilty conscience* which I probably should not have been alone in having.

Camus wanted to raise the consciousness of his *pieds-noirs* readers but diplomatically, by emphasizing his own guilty conscience and extending the hope that others would react in a similar fashion to the plight of the Kabyle.

The articles were also an attempt to reach out to the mostly *pieds-noirs* readership in a different way, by stating that Kabylia and Algeria as a whole were France's responsibility, because Algeria was a country, Camus writes, 'we made our own'—an understatement for the occupation of Algeria. In the last sentence of this same article, Camus declared that the task of the French was to provide for the needs and obligations of the Kabyle—a view which would much later be criticized as paternalistic by many Kabylians. However, at the time of publication Camus's articles were taken as a cry for help—asking for infrastructure funding for Kabylia.

Notwithstanding the later reaction of Algerian intellectuals, in the West and particularly in France, 'The misery of Kabylia' has been and continues to be described as a series of 'anti-colonialist' articles. It led to a perception that Camus was anti-colonialist himself. It is true that he wanted the Kabyle people to have better living conditions, a better life expectancy, better salaries and education, but all under the authority of the French Empire, something Camus never challenged. Camus wanted to reform colonialism, not abolish it.

Nevertheless, Camus's commitment in favour of better conditions for Arabs and Berbers antagonized the French colonial authorities. In fact, Camus's journalistic activism for colonial reform was one of the reasons French authorities eventually denied funding to *Alger républicain* and shut it down—though the newspaper's pacifist stance was the main reason. The paper published its last issue in September 1939, but its sister publication, *Soir républicain,* continued. It was obvious to Pia and Camus that their days as newspapermen in French Algeria were numbered. Not only politicians in Algeria and Paris but *pied-noir* public opinion and local authorities were opposed to any reform of the colonial system—however modest.

Camus feared that because of the intractability of the *pieds-noirs* authorities, proponents of a more radical solution—Algerian independence—would prevail. The *pieds-noirs* wanted to share nothing and, indeed, slightly more than twenty years later, they would be left with nothing. In the interim, Camus resolved to avoid the issue. His theory of the absurd—that the world made no sense and was unexplainable—can certainly be seen in his stance regarding political reform in Algeria; he stopped trying to change things, or indeed to make sense of them.

## Against the war

On the eve of the Second World War, Pia and Camus expressed support for the Munich Agreements and were in favour of peace with Hitler. This view was not popular with the authorities, which censored many of Camus's articles on the subject. Camus explained his point of view in an article styled 'Our position'. In it, he supported negotiations with Hitler as the only way to weaken what he saw as the German leader's prestige. For Camus, the source of Hitler's popularity resided mainly with the unjust Versailles treaty (which inflicted massive financial obligations on Germany as reparation to France and England after the First World War). Camus wrote that some of Hitler's claims were justified, and though he did not agree with the invasions of Poland and Czechoslovakia, he did not feel they warranted a war. His pacifism may have been linked to the death of his father in the

First World War; certainly the fear of carnage motivated him as it did most French citizens. This fear and lassitude was a widely shared view in France at the time and is often cited as one of the contributing causes to France's sudden defeat.

Camus and Pia's position—appeasement toward Hitler—quickly became harder to defend. Faced with governmental censorship and virulent attacks from competing newspapers, Camus cited support for his position by the British government and press. In one of the last articles Camus penned on the topic of war, he wrote a letter to an anonymous young Englishman in which he praised the man's restraint and lucidity, a way of supporting pacifism. In these articles, written in his own defence, Camus rejected the communist label and stated: 'we are resolutely pacifist'. His refusal to take a stand against Hitler was influenced by his own brand of nihilism, which he would develop in his play *Caligula*, published after the Second World War. Meanwhile he signed many of his pacifist articles under the pseudonym 'Nero' (another psychopathic Roman emperor). Yet Camus's nihilism was tinged with idealism since he believed that the advent of a European war would prove that nationalism was to be condemned.

The Germans attacked France in May 1940. The French army was quickly and resoundingly defeated. The Wehrmacht occupied Paris by mid-June. In July 1940, a vast majority of members of the French parliament voted for the end of the Third Republic and the transfer of full powers to Marshal Pétain, who wanted to make peace with Hitler. France was divided in two zones, one occupied by Germany (which comprised all of the western and northern coasts as well as Paris), and the other governed by the collaborationist government based in the small spa town of Vichy. This included, importantly for Camus, the Mediterranean coast and its access to Algeria. Travel was easier in this so-called free zone, though Camus would navigate between the two zones throughout the war.

Jobless, Camus once again had to find a way to survive. Given a recommendation from Pia he went to work for *Paris-soir*, a low-brow daily paper he despised. Camus lived in Paris in a small hotel room and worked on his writing. After the German invasion, *Paris-soir* relocated to the free zone, in Lyon. Camus then asked his fiancée, Francine Faure, who had finished her studies and was now a substitute maths teacher, to join him from Algeria and they were married in Lyon in December. It was a simple wedding: Pia and workers from the paper were the witnesses and sole participants. Unfortunately, during the occupation nothing was certain. Paper rationing resulted in huge cutbacks, and Camus was let go. With no employment prospects, he and Francine reluctantly moved back to Algeria to his wife's family home in Oran: they had nowhere else to go.

## The resistance and *Letters to a German Friend*

After struggling for a year and a half in Oran, a town he disliked, unable to find a steady job, and in seriously deteriorating health, Camus decided on doctor's advice to return to France and spend some time in the mountain air to recuperate. By August 1942 he was in a small village near Saint-Étienne called Le Panelier. Camus planned to return to his wife in Algeria after a few months in the mountains. However, after the USA landed in North Africa in November 1942, the German army invaded the French free zone and France became land-locked. Lines of communication were cut between France and Algeria. Albert and Francine were forcefully separated until her return to Paris in September 1944. Camus spent the summer of 1943 in Le Panelier. He was bored, did not like the company of the villagers, and missed Algeria. He also missed Francine, but not only her: he asked an old girlfriend, Blanche Balain, to come and visit him. He spent most of his time working on his second novel, *The Plague*, between visits to Lyon, Saint-Étienne, and, more rarely, Paris. Though he knew in the summer of 1943 that Pascal Pia and the famous poet Francis

Ponge (with whom Camus had been corresponding) were involved in resistance activities, which mainly consisted of publishing small, clandestine papers which denounced the occupation, Camus did not join them. He would join the resistance in December 1943 or January 1944, some eight months before the liberation of Paris in August of 1944. He joined a group, including Pia and Ponge, which was publishing one of the first and most important underground resistance newspapers, *Combat* (see Figure 3).

*Combat* was initially under the control of resisters who thought Marshal Pétain was playing a double game with Germany and was on their side. Pia lent his experience as an editor and newspaper publisher, and Camus wrote articles and editorials, most of them after the liberation. His first action for the resistance consisted

3. In the editorial offices of French resistance paper *Combat*, 1944: l–r: Petit Breton (uniform), Victor Peroni, Albert Camus, Albert Ollivier (smoking), Jean Bloch-Michel (small, profile), Jean Chauveau (profile drinking), Roger Grenier (face, glasses), Pascal Pia, Henri Calet, Francois Bruel, Serge Karsky; foreground: Marcelle Rapinat and Charlotte Rau.

in writing his four 'Letters to a German Friend', only two of which were published from January to August 1944 in underground publications. These short essays are significant because they describe what Camus thought the resistance was about and his rationale for joining it when he did.

Imagine two friends in a room: one French, one German; the Frenchman does all of the talking—that is the setting for Camus's 'Letters to a German Friend'. These are not really letters, but rather monologues with an imaginary German friend as an audience who rarely speaks and, when he does, only through Camus (a technique that he will employ many years later in his novel *The Fall*).

In the first letter Camus explained 'the reasons for the delay': by which he meant generally the delay in France's response to the German invasion. According to Camus, this delay was motivated by a search for a rationale. He put forth the notion of an enlightened patriotism that needed reasons to go to war beyond patriotism. The French were suspicious of heroism, Camus tells his German friend: 'we were still learning to conquer our doubts about heroism. I know, you think we are strangers to heroism. You are wrong.' It took some time for France to overcome its doubts about heroism, and that was why France lost and why, after the defeat, so few resisted immediately. But he was also indirectly explaining his own path to the resistance and justifying his earlier pacifism.

In the second letter, he again explained France's defeat and the delay to resist in larger numbers: 'we took the time to find our reasons'. Camus dated this delay from the start of the war; it took three years to combine nationalism with the pursuit of equity and justice. This viewpoint, that the resistance had to have a social component, would be a constant theme for the movement and for its representatives after the war. The resistance after the war wanted to herald a new era in French politics and *Combat* was to be at the forefront of this new struggle.

In the third letter, Camus launched into a defence of Europe, and wrote that the very word 'Europe' was sullied by its association with Nazism. Camus claimed that Germany started to see Europe as a land of conquest 'starting with the day you lost Africa' (speaking to his imaginary German friend). In many ways, Nazi Germany treated France as a colony during the occupation. At that time, Camus and the French people living under German rule were objectively closer to the normal living conditions of Algerians under French rule. Further linking colonial status to power and prestige, Camus wrote that France's superiority over Germany was that the former was a colonial power. Camus clearly believed that the key to France's prestige and power was its colonies.

The fourth letter was even more personal. In it, Camus stated that he shared the same values as those of his German friend—namely, that the world had no meaning, a reference to the absurd and nihilism. From this starting point, where good and evil are equivalent, the German chose to dive into war and conquest whereas Camus opposed 'France's violent taste for justice'. Camus was angry at Germany for 'forcing' France to 'enter History'.

(In his articles for *Combat*, Camus came to terms with history and the necessity to be part of it; by late 1943, Camus probably understood that not to join the resistance, which his friends had already done, would doom his literary career. By the time Paris was liberated, Camus was one of its main public voices. Camus was now living in Paris permanently. His wife Francine had joined him from Algiers, and would give birth to their twin children, Catherine and Jean, on 5 September 1945.)

## Camus, resistance editorialist

Between March and July of 1944 Camus wrote—but did not sign for obvious reasons—a total of six short pieces (though opinions differ among scholars as to how many of these are actually by Camus) for the underground version of *Combat*. These were propaganda pieces, denouncing the Wehrmacht's violence and the Gestapo's use of torture and attacking Pétain, his prime minister Pierre Laval, and the French pro-German militias. The general thrust of the pieces was a call to unity and a warning to collaborators that they would be judged and punished once the war ended.

Immediately following the liberation of Paris in August 1944, the next series of articles by Camus had a similar tone, though more inclusive and less combative. Camus wanted all factions of the resistance to join together in a show of national unity. This aim and the generally positive and open tone were crucial in a country which was torn apart by the war and which in its great majority did not resist the Nazi occupiers. The actions of the average French citizens preoccupied with earning a living should be contrasted to those of the elites, nearly all of whom eagerly backed Pétain as soon as he came to power. In fact, nearly 90 per cent of members of parliament backed Pétain.

To salvage France's past and preserve its future, the fictional story of a France composed mostly of resisters had to be told. Intellectuals would play a crucial role in this enterprise as the tellers of this story, as its beneficiaries, but also sometimes as its victims. There was an unspoken consensus, from the non-communist left to the followers of General de Gaulle, and from virtually all literary circles, to grant the title of *résistant* to just about anyone who had not overtly collaborated. This consensus took the form of an idealization of the immediate past which was echoed in the rhetoric of Camus's *Combat* articles.

Camus became a sort of public spokesperson for the resistance; he certainly would speak for it in his editorials in *Combat* after the liberation. The tone in his first editorials was that of the moral arbiter of the times, making grand pronouncements on France and its past, present, and future course of action. Camus had to fight for that title: he engaged the famous novelist Mauriac in a debate on whether French collaborators should be vigorously punished. He famously said, in regard to enemies of the resistance, that there needed to be more figures like Saint-Just—a historic hero from the French revolution who, along with his ally Robespierre, was in favour of the death penalty for the enemies of the Revolution. However, Camus would change his mind only a few months later; after having seen what he thought were the excesses of the *épuration*, or purging, he came to oppose the death penalty and to agree with Mauriac.

Camus had other concerns: he was against a return to a Third Republic dominated by money. Camus wrote that Germans forced the French to kill or live on their knees and concluded by saying that the French are not a race to live kneeling. The article climaxed heroically: 'on 21 August 1944, in the streets of Paris, a struggle began which for all of us and for all of France will end with freedom or death'.

Here too, Camus contributed to the myth created largely by Charles de Gaulle—the myth of France as a major force in the fight against Nazi Germany. The liberation of Paris was meant as a show of force to bolster the morale of Parisians. In fact, de Gaulle asked the Americans if General Leclerc's armoured divisions could liberate Paris and this was the subject of fairly intense negotiations. Although Leclerc's tanks did enter Paris first, it was the anglophone landing in Normandy, made possible by the Soviet Union's massive pressure on the Wehrmacht on the eastern front, that led to Paris's liberation. But when de Gaulle entered the City of Light, he gave a famous speech proclaiming that Paris had freed itself, and by extension the idea that France would free itself as well.

This rhetoric was part of what de Gaulle saw as crucial myth-making to save France's unity, to reinstil a modicum of pride in a thoroughly demoralized people. The 'honour' of France—and the credibility of its leadership—would also be restored through a reframing of the actions of its intellectuals. There was to be no middle ground: you were either a collaborator or a resister, even though the reality was highly complex and ambiguous.

Camus himself played a substantial part in this myth-making, especially right after the liberation of Paris, in his first published articles, which had titles such as: 'The blood of freedom', 'The night of truth', and 'The time for disdain'. In those editorials, he justified, even glorified, liberating violence. This language befitted the celebrations that took place all over France on VE Day (Victory in Europe Day). This was to be the final purge before the dawning of a new era of peace. But not so in Algeria.

The occasion of VE Day and the celebration led some Algerians to unfurl and wave the Algerian flag—after all, many of them were front-line veterans of the very first victory of the remnants of the French army on the Italian front. The French police responded to these demonstrations by shooting at the demonstrators. This response gave rise to greater riots, during which about 100 French policemen and *pieds-noirs* were killed.

The French and *pieds-noirs* reaction led to one of the darkest and least talked about episodes in French history. For weeks on end, French police and armed forces alongside *pieds-noirs* militias systematically and indiscriminately massacred thousands of Algerians, especially at Sétif and Guelma. The French air force bombed entire villages, razing them to the ground. Back in Paris, the metropolitan press in its vast majority ignored the massacres. But not so Albert Camus.

Since most of France was effectively liberated by the end of 1944, Camus was free to travel. He had just returned from an extensive trip in Algeria, during which time he had drafted articles to describe the plight of Arabs to French readers and to explain that the French had to conquer Algeria 'a second time', by which he meant that France had to win the hearts and minds of the Arabs and Berbers. In light of this objective, the massacres at Sétif and Guelma undid whatever Camus was hoping to see done—just as his articles were to be published. Though he could not pretend the massacres did not happen, he minimized them. It bears noting that in Camus's perspective, it was the Algerians who committed massacres; he described the systematic killing of thousands of Algerians by the colonizing forces by using the more neutral term 'repression'. In his own words:

> The massacres of Guelma and Sétif provoked the indignation and a deep-felt resentment in the French of Algeria. The repression that followed gave rise to a feeling of fear and hostility for the Arab masses.

The choice of words here is interesting. Camus described the emotions of the *pieds-noirs* as those of victims: 'indignation' and 'resentment', whereas for the 'Arab masses' the feelings were of an instinctive nature: 'fear' and 'hostility'. Even when describing the massacres at Sétif and Guelma, Camus could not help but betray where his sympathies lay.

Thus, the mass killing of Algerians by the French authorities and *pieds-noirs* rated only a few inaccurate lines in Camus's article. Perhaps Camus was aware that widespread knowledge of these state-sponsored crimes would destroy the credibility of France's image as a benevolent and enlightened empire. Certainly, to this day, the massacres at Sétif and Guelma are a taboo subject in French history; they are rarely discussed and largely absent from history books. Nevertheless, these massacres were the beginning of the end for the French occupation of Algeria. Less than ten years later, the war for Algerian independence began.

## Hiroshima

Three months to the day after VE Day and the start of the Algerian massacres, US planes dropped an atomic bomb on Hiroshima, instantly killing 80,000 people. In the French press there was a chorus of celebrations and positive comments. Camus, alone among his peers in journalism and in the French literary world, was unequivocal in his condemnation: 'industrial civilization has just reached the ultimate stage of savagery'. And Camus went on to condemn science as well:

> That in a world left incapable of any restraint, left to all the sorrows of violence, indifferent to justice and to the simple happiness of men, that in this world science would devote itself to organized murder, no one—short of being an impenitent idealist—would think to be surprised.

This mood of general disillusion pervaded intellectual circles in the aftermath of the Second World War. The German philosopher and thinker Theodor Adorno famously said that after Auschwitz it would be impossible to write poetry. How could one not reject science after Hiroshima? asked Camus. In fact, his disenchantment with science pre-dated the war. Camus's rejection of any all-explaining narrative, be it communism, religion, science, or simply human history, was at the centre of his theory of the absurd, which he developed during his years as a journalist.

# Chapter 3
# Camus and the absurd

What is the absurd? Have you ever felt a sense of uneasiness when you wondered where you were, a moment when you lost all frame of reference with regard to time, space, and history? A sudden—but often fleeting—onset of doubt about the meaning of all things? That feeling was the absurd for Camus. In his seminal essay on the absurd, *The Myth of Sisyphus*, he described the occurrence of this feeling at the sight of a man on the other side of a café window, talking animatedly to a telephone: Camus could not hear him and this vision of another human earnestly speaking to a piece of plastic set things in motion. The profound sense of unease he felt as a result was one of the manifestations of the absurd.

The absurd is a feeling that comes out of experience. For Camus it was a near-death experience: the brutal onset of tuberculosis at the age of 17. From that point on, and throughout his life, Camus's health was frail, and he often had to take weeks, if not months, off from work to stave off or recuperate from the disease. His illness was a constant reminder that all social pursuits could become meaningless at any time. Marriage, work, justice, religion, and knowledge are all challenged by the feeling of the absurd. This awareness of the certainty of death set him apart from people around him going about their lives actively ignoring their mortality. In this aspect, the absurd and existentialism are alike:

at their core is an awareness of mortality and the centrality of human beings (over religion for example). However, for existentialists this feeling of the absurd is only a starting point: feelings of existential uncertainty are to be transcended by art, or through human responsibility and collective engagement with the world. For Camus, the feeling of the absurd is an end unto itself and is not to be transcended, but accepted and embraced.

The absurd convinced Camus that there is no meaning to life because it could be cut short at any moment. From that starting point, Camus had to come to terms with what he saw as the impossibility of explaining or making sense of both life and death. Camus called this resolution to face the absurdity of life 'the will of the absurd'—a willingness to accept one's mortality and one's inability to comprehend life. Therefore, the absurd is both the realization of a situation and a changed consciousness, an awakening, a decision to face a meaningless world. He would express this to the poet Francis Ponge in the summer of 1943: 'the feeling of the absurd is the world that is dying, the will of the absurd is the new world'.

The 'world that is dying' is the world of traditional explanations (religions, philosophies that attempt to make sense of life). Camus casts aside these beliefs and systems of thought. The 'new world' is the goal of a world with a new consciousness, an awareness and an acceptance of the absurd. In his writings, Camus offered examples of that new consciousness in which nature, especially the sun, and none more than the Algerian sun, features prominently. Camus had to use stories to illustrate both the feeling and the will of the absurd, because both are rooted in experience. The two absurds are the matrix behind his narrative drive at this stage in his writing life.

His first three major works, *Caligula*, *The Stranger*, and *The Myth of Sisyphus*, were about narrating the absurd experiences, and the sometime violent clashes between those awakened to the absurdity of life and those who choose to ignore it. Camus called these works 'my three absurds'. Each work stages the absurd uniquely. In the play *Caligula*, the Roman emperor experiences the feeling of the absurd and sets out to teach it forcibly to his subjects. In the novel *The Stranger*, the reader is directly targeted and made to feel the absurd. Lastly, in *The Myth of Sisyphus*, Camus illustrates, through narratives and examples, the will of the absurd.

## Caligula

*Caligula* is Camus's first play. He started to write it in 1937 and finished it in 1939, but it was not staged until the autumn of 1944, weeks after the liberation of Paris. Along with Nero, Caligula has been depicted as the archetype of the mad tyrant. However, Camus's play is not the typical tale of resistance to oppression: the opposition to Caligula is motivated by his subjects' desire to lead a life undisturbed by metaphysical questioning. The play is about the absurd and to what lengths people will go to avoid facing it. It is a confrontation between Caligula, who is aware of the absurd, and his subjects, who would rather ignore it.

While reading or watching the play, it is hard for one to feel outright sympathy or complete distaste for either Caligula or his subjects, and that is one of Camus's objectives. The reader oscillates uncomfortably between moments of empathy for Caligula's victims and feelings of disdain for their hypocrisy. This discomfort exists to make readers question themselves, their belief systems, and everything they take for granted—including the need to identify with a character. These feelings of unease and uncertainty are two of the manifestations of the feeling of the absurd. Camus will employ this technique of estrangement even more prominently in *The Stranger*.

At the beginning of the play, Caligula experiences a crisis after the death of his sister (and lover). Caligula is distraught not so much by her death but by the realization that his grief will pass. He feels intense sadness while he simultaneously realizes that it will fade through no will of his own. This experience leads him to become aware of the absurdity of existence. Caligula returns to Rome a changed man, determined to teach this lesson to his subjects, and so he starts to randomly mistreat them.

*Caligula* is a pedagogical play: convinced of the absurdity of the world, Caligula decides to demonstrate it. His teachings include rape, psychological torture, murder—all applied randomly. For example, in one scene, Caligula kills a citizen on a false suspicion, and by way of justification after realizing his mistake he whispers 'sooner or later', referring to the certainty of death. Caligula's crimes are a means to an end: to demonstrate to his subjects the arbitrariness of life. Caligula's actions towards his subjects are much like Camus's toward his readers: he inflicts upon them the absurd with all its injustices and randomness. Caligula's targets are many. The play consists of a series of lessons about the futility of various beliefs and values that Caligula's subjects hold dear. His main targets are patricians (technically aristocrats or noblemen, though in the first version of the play they were to be senators). Certainly, they represent the privileged class, the property owners, though many of Caligula's actions affect the larger population as well.

One such lesson takes place when Caligula decides to force the wealthy to change their wills and leave their fortunes to the state; all then must put their names on a list, and some will be executed at random. Caligula pointedly notes that everyone will be condemned to death anyway: judges, the public, the jury, everyone. Caligula chooses to act like the gods to demonstrate how arbitrary and cruel they are. He is also challenging the gods to strike him down, and in his mind his continued existence is the proof of the gods' indifference.

*Caligula* would express pure nihilism were it not for the presence of a hero of sorts: Cherea, a patrician intellectual who is against

Caligula but refuses to join the plot to kill him. His is an unexpected voice—the incarnation of a middle ground between unsympathetic victims and the bold tyrant. Cherea understands the absurd and what Caligula is trying to do but is against his anti-humanist rhetoric and violence.

Camus drafted different versions of the play, and Cherea's role becomes more significant with every version. The increased presence of Cherea corresponds to Camus's changing position on the absurd. Cherea incarnates Camus's awareness that the absurd must somehow combine with some sort of moral framework lest it become pure nihilism. Camus modified Cherea's character in later versions to include lines in which he is determined to fight against 'a great idea whose triumph would mean the end of the world'—a clear nod to the fight against Nazism.

However, in the original 1939 version, during a confrontation with Caligula, Cherea tells his emperor that he thinks some actions are more beautiful than others. Caligula responds that all human actions are equivalent and Cherea replies: 'I understand and agree with you.' Camus excised this last line with its moral relativism from the 1944 version of the play. In the context of France's liberation (when the play was first staged), Camus had to change the original version lest Cherea's reply seem like an apology for tyrants. Paradoxically, the original 1939 version was not staged during the occupation for the opposite reason: it might have seemed like a veiled attack on Hitler.

Camus modified *Caligula* many times because of the changing historical context. It is an ironic fate for a play that Camus meant to express the most pure, nihilistic version of the absurd. Cherea's presence and moderating stance represented a toned down absurd, and pointed to Camus's changing view: the absurd in all of its nihilistic purity was no longer defensible—certainly not after Hitler. The Second World War and its moral aftermath led Camus to inject a degree of moralism and humanism into his thought, which then led to his notion of revolt, the subject of his second cycle of works.

Although this interpretation became consensual, when the play was first presented in September of 1945, many critics thought it too soft on Caligula, and conflated the mad emperor's nihilism with Camus's own beliefs, much to his annoyance and despite his recent article condemning the bombing of Hiroshima.

## *The Stranger* and the absurd

In August 1937 Camus jotted down the following notes in his diary for *The Stranger*:

> [the story of] a man who had sought life where most people find it (marriage, career, etc.) and who suddenly notices, while reading a fashion catalogue, how foreign he has been to his own life (life as it is seen in fashion catalogues).

Originally a fashion catalogue was a handbook of costumes for various social positions. Today they are at the heart of consumer culture. In this novel, along with Catholic rituals, Camus rejects the bourgeoisie and its values for the role they play in this absurd world. This stance will be a huge part of the appeal for many generations of readers, for *The Stranger* introduces a different kind of character in French fiction: the office worker. This relatively new social status, a new social category, is at the centre of the novel.

*The Stranger*, set in 1930s French Algeria, is divided into two parts. The first is the story of Meursault, a young office worker. Upon the death of his mother, Meursault does not feel anything and does not understand that society would like him to display emotions. The famous opening sentences of the novel, universally interpreted as a statement of indifference toward the death of his mother, took the French literary establishment by storm:

> Mother died today. Or yesterday maybe, I don't know. I got a telegram from the retirement home. 'Mother deceased. Funeral tomorrow. Faithfully yours.' That doesn't mean anything. Maybe it was yesterday.

As instructed by the retirement home, Meursault goes to the funeral the next day. The following day he returns home and goes to the movies and sleeps with a former colleague. He also helps a pimp take revenge on a woman. The following weekend, he goes to the beach with a few friends where, after an altercation, he inexplicably—'because of the sun' he says at his trial—shoots a young Arab man five times, killing him.

The second part of the novel deals with Meursault's imprisonment and trial. Although his attorney expected a light sentence, Meursault now risks the death penalty, not for killing an Arab but for his refusal to mourn his mother. He is prosecuted for his 'strangeness', for his active indifference and refusal to conform to the foundational values of French society: respect for one's parents, marriage, and the pursuit of professional success. Meursault has lived his life as though acutely aware of the absurd nature of our collective existence, and this awareness has made him indifferent to all values and, as such, a danger to society.

In the end, it is as society would have it: Meursault is sentenced to be guillotined in a public place. Yet the plot is far-fetched from the very start; no French settler was ever sentenced to death for the killing of an Arab in colonial Algeria. The plot is an excuse; the death of the Arab, a means to an end: it is French bourgeois society which is put on trial by Camus, through its rituals, its habits, its presuppositions. French accepted values are challenged—with the notable, but rarely noted, exception of those pertaining to colonialism.

44

Meursault puts the ritual of mourning in question with the opening sentences of the novel in which he professes not to remember the date of his mother's death and then points out the vacuity of conventions. By juxtaposing a shocking statement ('I don't remember when my mother died') with a more consensual one (standardized but meaningless expressions such as 'faithfully yours'), Meursault destabilizes the reader. The reader's 'respectable' self is shocked by Meursault's directness but also sympathizes with a few of Meursault's attacks on convention—thus alternatively agreeing with and faulting the character.

The first part of the novel challenges the rites of mourning, but later sections question social ambitions, friendship, the justice system, and marriage, to name but a few. Meursault and the reader begin to realize that bourgeois society is demanding a drama of explicit expression of these roles—the grieving son, the loving husband, and so on. Rejecting these roles leads to suspicion from other members of society. Meursault is therefore a suspect before he has committed any crimes.

Another example occurs after Meursault returns to work, when his boss asks him how old his mother was:

> I worked hard at the office today. The boss was nice. He asked me if I wasn't too tired and he also wanted to know Mother's age. I said 'About sixty', so as to not make a mistake; and I don't know why, but he seemed to be relieved somehow and to consider the matter closed.

The paradox here is that although Meursault does not remember his mother's age, he is acutely aware of the importance of appearances and is afraid that his boss might be scandalized by an honest answer. This fear plays to the conventional expectations of the reader. But to the surprise of Meursault, his boss is relieved by his vague response. He probably doesn't want to know his mother's age, only that she was old enough for her death not to be considered tragic. The boss is relieved because her death was normal, in conformity with the expectations of society. In short, the question posed by his boss is not in any way indicative of genuine concern for another, paralleling how circumstantial questions after a tragic event can be devoid of meaning. Meursault's indifference is also a reaction to the other characters of the novel, who are, as is the conventional reader, 'perfectly integrated into society'—the very definition of conformity.

Behaving well is also upholding the new bourgeois social order. This precept makes us wonder—who is the Stranger? Is it Meursault, who tells the truth, or is it we the readers who cover up and neutralize our emotions and our indifference with words? This subtle process enables us to look back on what we thought were our own moral values and discover that they are only the product of a collective moral code. In doing so, we begin to liberate ourselves from that moral code and face the meaninglessness of the world.

Camus takes on marriage through Meursault, who is spending time with a former co-worker. She asks him to marry her, and he responds with characteristic indifference:

> That evening Marie came by to see me and asked me if I wanted to marry her. I said it didn't make any difference to me and that we could if she wanted to. Then she wanted to know if I loved her. I answered the same way I had the last time, that it didn't mean anything but that I probably didn't love her.

Here again Meursault does not attack marriage directly. He accepts Marie's proposal while simultaneously denying its importance. Once more Meursault undermines societal values by both agreeing and questioning.

Meursault seems to display a radical, almost intractable, indifference to almost everything the rest of the characters are concerned with (love, work, social rites). What is at the root of this indifference? Often indifference is a defence mechanism, a reaction to shattering disappointment or disillusion. If we look at Camus's own life, there are events which could shed light on Meursault's reaction, particularly in regard to Meursault's indifference to professional ambition. His words about giving up his studies and work ambitions resonate with Camus's own experiences. He studied for many years at university and wrote a thesis only to be rejected by the French state doctors as permanently ineligible to teach in the French educational system because of his health. Here Meursault might have been talking about Camus's feelings when reflecting on his past ambitions: 'When I was a student, I had lots of ambitions like that. But when I had to give up my studies I learned very quickly that none of it really mattered.' On some level, Camus must have viewed his years of university work as meaningless. And Camus's ambivalence at the funeral of his maternal grandmother in which he felt little grief and cried to conform can certainly be linked to the opening paragraph of the novel. We can also connect his failed marriage with Simone Hié as having influenced his depiction of Meursault's position on marriage. He transferred personal experiences of radical discomfort or disappointment and his resulting indifference onto his fiction.

Other interpretations framed Meursault's indifference as a critique of society's intolerance towards those who do not conform. For Sartre, Meursault's lack of awareness of moral codes made him resemble Candide, the anti-hero of Voltaire's most famous *conte philosophique*. Critic and philosopher Roland Barthes (1915–80) focused on the purity of the style in *The Stranger* and considered it a function of Meursault's indifference.

Yet Meursault's indifference is not all encompassing. It follows the absurd logic of the novel that his only friend, Raymond Sintès, is a pimp. As an absurd man has no morals, so Raymond's profession does not bother Meursault. When Sintès beats a woman so savagely that her screams lead to the arrival of the police, Meursault provides false testimony to cover for his friend. Gone is the automatic benevolence of the main character which typically occurs in novels. Meursault seemingly lives a life void of morality.

Meursault and Sintès have something in common: their intense dislike of the police. Their hatred of the police is a revelation that society is the enemy, but it is not immediately clear which segment of society is targeted. It is important to know that in the context of colonial Algeria, the police are the hated representative of the Parisian central authority, the metropole. Meursault and Sintès bond around their identity as *pieds-noirs*: indifferent to Arab life and actively resentful of the mainland French.

That unity against Arabs manifests itself on many occasions in the novel, though never more clearly than when Meursault kills the young Arab man. The action takes place on the beach in Algiers. After a fight pitting Meursault, Sintès, and a friend of Sintès against three Algerian men which saw the retreat of the *pieds-noirs*, Meursault returns to the scene of the fight. He sees an Arab man lying down playing the flute. In perhaps the most famous scene of the book—in which the sun and the heat play a prominent role—Meursault walks toward the man, who shows Meursault his knife. The sun's reflection on the knife projects onto Meursault's eyes. He then shoots the Arab five times. He is imprisoned and the trial that follows spans most of the second part of the novel. Oddly, the trial doesn't address Meursault's actual guilt, as none of the Arabs is asked to testify and the murder itself does not seem to concern the judicial machine.

The trial is an opportunity for Camus to denounce the French judiciary, but it also provides the stage from which Camus can denounce general bourgeois conformity. From the militantly religious judge who waves his crucifix in Meursault's face during the pre-trial proceedings and calls him an anti-Christ, to the incompetent defence lawyer and grandstanding prosecutor, the court system seems concerned mostly with its own reputation and the enforcement of conservative moral values. Ultimately the outcome of the trial hinges entirely on the morality of the accused.

With this focus, Meursault is in bad shape, given the lack of tears at his mother's funeral, his unawareness of her age, and his sleeping with a co-worker very soon thereafter. Here, too, Camus's life experiences are at the root of this disappointment: spending time as a journalist reporting trials, he often denounced the verdicts, sometimes even starting petitions in an attempt to reverse them. At the same time, however, it is French bourgeois society which is on trial here. Everyone in the courthouse is a model of conformity; everyone is playing a societal role to perfection. Ostensibly, the trial is there to point out the absurdity of the fact that Meursault is guilty not of killing another human being, but of not shedding tears at his mother's funeral. Yet, a mystery remains: why does Meursault kill the young Arab man?

Despites his overt indifference, there are some things Meursault quite likes. He enjoys food (and wine, and tobacco), and he is interested in Marie, though for purely physical reasons. Echoing the major leitmotif of Camus's heroes throughout his fiction, Meursault adores nature above all else. He only seems truly happy when describing the sea, the beach, and especially the sun. Meursault's interaction with nature is almost a merging with it. This communion with nature is another illustration of *bonheur*. Meursault is not interested in projecting himself into the future (refusal of promotion, marriage)—he lives in the present, for the moment.

The sun and its light, which Meursault worships throughout the novel, embody this special relationship to nature, which some commentators have called sacred. These moments of communion with nature provide an escape from time as measured by humans, an escape from the past, from history and collective memory.

The depiction of nature in *The Stranger* reflects a major difference between the views of Camus and those of Jean-Paul Sartre. In Sartrean existentialism, interactions with nature trigger moments of deep existential uncertainty but these moments are meant to be transcended through human activity. For Camus's absurd, interactions with nature are desirable and ultimately the sole source of solace.

In regard to the murder, one interpretation is that Meursault kills the Arab man because he has interfered with his interaction with nature. By making himself comfortable, lying down on the beach, the young man is symbolically reclaiming that space (he is 'making himself at home'). Then he symbolically captures the sun and shines the reflection of his knife on Meursault's face. Given his love of nature and of the sun, this is something of a sacrilege for Meursault.

Many commentators, such as Conor Cruise O'Brien and Edward Said, have written on the absence of Arabs as named, speaking human beings in the novel. The absence of Arab and Berber life in the novel is odd since Camus was obviously aware of and concerned by the colonial situation and wrote extensively about the Kabyle people's plight. There seems to be a formal reticence—Camus did not want his novel to be an overtly colonial one (which perhaps paradoxically for some readers ensured that it would be). He wrote it as a mechanism to obscure the place in history of Algeria, a strategy for insisting on the metaphysical issues relating to absurdity rather than on colonialism. This is symbolized by the murder of the Arab man, which seems almost a pretext for a discussion of philosophical issues deemed more important than the murder, and its nameless victim.

Other commentators, such as Robert Zaretsky and David Carroll, disagree with O'Brien and consider that Meursault's exclusion from society gives him similar status to an Arab, and that, being stripped of his humanity, Meursault ultimately becomes the other, the excluded.

Yet, Camus's actual description of Arabs in this, his most famous novel, is disturbing. Perhaps we can look back at his profound disappointment at France's refusal to share power with a small number of Algerian elites. The complete failure of the compromise Blum–Viollette bill, which, if enacted, would have accomplished this modest goal, occurred before Camus finished his novel. Behind the anonymous, indifferent description of Arabs lies Camus's dashed dream of a path toward a more just and equitable French presence in Algeria. In *The Stranger*, Camus represses any issue he may have had with colonialism. He takes to task a host of societal values—love, friendship, work, justice—but not the oppression of Arabs. It is as though Camus has given up on this crucial issue and decided to repress it. In the process he indirectly ratifies the colonial order by leaving it in the background.

## The Myth of Sisyphus

Camus's *Myth of Sisyphus* is an essay that changes in style and focus as it progresses. It is a discussion of philosophical ideas, a description of feelings; sometimes it reads like a lamentation, sometimes like a lyrical ode. It is a blueprint on how to live an absurd life; it is an intelligent attack on intelligence. As such it is hard to pin down.

In a short introductory note Camus warns us: this text will not be about an absurd philosophy, but about an absurd sensibility. Yet in the opening sentence of the essay he writes: 'There is only one really important philosophical problem: it is suicide', squarely putting himself in in the realm of philosophy. Camus uses this opening to introduce us to his feeling of the absurd, which will dominate the first part of the essay. The opening statement regards a person faced with the realization that life is devoid of meaning except for the certainty of death. Would not suicide—one's own decision, after all—be the ultimate act of human agency? Camus says no, the absurd is a result of the unsettling confrontation between one's quest for meaning and life's meaninglessness; he advises his readers to embrace it. The realization that life is finite should lead one to live one's life to the absolute fullest; therefore, premature death via suicide is an obstacle, not a solution. Camus states that he cannot define the absurd but rather must enumerate the feelings that contain the absurd and the situations that give rise to it: for example, when he stares at a stone, this 'thickness, this strangeness of the world, that's the absurd'.

These feelings of the absurd are not to be resolved or transcended, not even explained. In *The Myth of Sisyphus* Camus attacks the notion of knowledge, of science, of explanations of any kind. Some of the most telling statements in the essay are assertions by Camus: 'reason is blind', 'universal reason is laughable'. He goes on to state that he is against all-explaining theories and embraces what he sees as an irreconcilable divorce (his word) between the irrational and his desire for clarity. His will of the absurd is an awareness and acceptance of the feeling of the absurd as a starting point to live an absurd life. In the second part of the essay, Camus describes and praises noteworthy examples of absurd lives.

An awareness of the absurdity is liberating; that is one of Camus's central tenets in *The Myth of Sisyphus*. Refusing to build a system of thought, he stakes out a way of life for the absurd man (there is not a single example of an absurd woman), which features the required outlook, role models, and ideal professions. Camus now writes of himself in the first person, as an example of the absurd man: 'The doctrines that explain everything make me irresponsible, make me weaker: one has to die reconciled to the idea of death, not of one's free will.' In the meantime, Camus suggests, live life to the fullest but as an individual, not part of a collective: 'I can only experience my own freedom.'

The absurd man 'enjoys a freedom from common rules'. How so? First, the absurd man is indifferent to the future, lives for the moment. He has a passion to take all that is given and has no deep-seated sense of values, since having those would give meaning to a life he knows is meaningless. And, consequently, the absurd life is about living more as opposed to living better. This declaration Camus illustrates with the character of Don Juan: 'If Don Juan leaves a woman it is absolutely not because he no longer desires her. A beautiful woman is always desirable. But it is because he desires another and *no* it is not the same thing...' Here, Camus puts himself forward as an expert witness to emphatically explain Don Juan's motivations. Was Camus a Don Juan? His personal life would tend to confirm it. He had numerous liaisons, including during his second marriage. After the war, when friends came from out of town to visit, they would often call Francine (his wife) to ask for the number of his current mistress—since that was the best way to find him. This was extremely distressing to Francine, and Camus told everyone (including his mistresses) how guilty he felt. Yet they stayed together until his death.

Another example concerns theatre actors, whom he describes as uniquely absurd because of the ephemeral nature of their work. The actor learns a role and lives someone else's life—usually heroic—to the fullest and then is on to the next life, the next role.

Camus idealizes the warriors, the Don Juans, the actors: they are all facing who they are, they are 'princes without kingdoms'—an echo of Baudelaire's comparison of the poet with the albatross, 'the prince of the skies'. Camus contrasts this elite, which includes himself, to 'sheep'—regular folks, unaware of the absurd, who are, in his words, 'cuckolded' by absurd men.

Only at the end of the essay does Camus return to his retelling of the myth of Sisyphus: a man sentenced by the gods to the absurd task of forever pushing this rock up a hill, only to see it fall back down every time he gets to the top. Sisyphus, Camus tells us, should be considered a happy person; that is, we should be aware of our plight and embrace whatever life we have to live on this earth to the fullest.

## The importance of *bonheur*

One of the ways to face the absurd consciously is to live a life with as many moments of privileged interaction with nature as possible, moments of *bonheur*. *Bonheur* speaks to bliss, time spent in nature, under the sun, by the beach, among the ruins, when Camus felt at one with the world and freed from a sense of time. The privileged site for his feeling, aside from the Algerian sun, was the Roman ruins in Tipasa.

In an early collection of essays published in Algiers in 1938, Camus recounts a day trip to Tipasa ('Nuptials in Tipasa'). In a densely lyrical text, Camus describes his moment of supreme unity with nature, which gives rise in him to feelings of love, and the sense of belonging to a 'race' which draws its greatness 'in its simplicity, standing on the beaches and sending knowing smiles to the skies' dazzling smile'. For all the grandiosity of the moment, it is temporary—Camus states that he would never stay more than a day there. Moments of *bonheur* are self-contained, short lived—then back to Algiers, back to his day job, like Sisyphus. In fact, the ethos of Camus, a life of work and dreariness interspersed with moments of communion with nature, oddly fits the office worker's average life, with long weeks of drudgery broken up by weekends. Camus codifies and mythologizes the new life of the employee, now with paid vacations, one of the great victories of the French labour movement.

Over a decade later, Camus is back in his beloved ruins and writes 'Return to Tipasa'; it is the same vibrant and lyrical expression of the irrevocable, primal connection Camus has with nature and this land—a connection which he calls love. Here is the absolute moment for the person aware of the absurd: unity with nature, rejection of civilization, reason, progress, and history. Of course, the irony here is that Tipasa was a colonial outpost of the Roman Empire. Although Camus wants to avoid human history and events, they keep coming; sometimes they manifest themselves from the outside, forcing changes in the text, as with *Caligula*, and sometimes they are part of the landscape, as in Tipasa.

Camus writes that life is meaningless but even meaninglessness lends it meaning. Thus, he gives meaninglessness a name. The notion of the absurd is a kind of contradiction, and Camus gives himself heroic status for noticing it and living in it. By advocating ignorance and the refusal of explanations as preconditions to happiness, Camus effectively theorizes his despair, which may have been caused by the intractable situation in colonial Algeria, and rationalizes his refusal to confront it. From here on, Camus rejects long-term political commitments and will intervene politically on a case-by-case basis.

The success and appeal of Camus's notion of the absurd are perhaps what gives his readers a way to feel—and live with—their unhappiness; this is a sort of metaphysical turn in Camus. He tells his readers to accept their unhappiness, to put it at the centre of their lives and use it to help them live a better one. In that sense the absurd becomes an ideology of individual acceptance which leaves out social and historical conflicts.

But, by the time Camus had finished *The Myth of Sisyphus*, human history had come roaring back, in the form of the Second World War. This led to serious changes in Camus's outlook. Soon the absurd would give way to the new Camusian notion of revolt.

# Chapter 4
# Rebel without a cause

In 1943, Camus wrote in his diary: 'to ask the question of the absurd world is to ask: "are we going to accept despair passively?" I suppose no honest person can say yes.' This early entry encapsulates his awareness that events were forcing him to transcend the nihilism of the absurd (Figure 4). In the midst of the Second World War, Camus realized that he could not be indifferent to the Nazi occupation of France and thus the nihilism of his absurd was untenable.

Camus was still firmly against all-explaining theories and systemic change, but he had to find a way to theorize and narrate his decision to join the resistance, which on many levels contradicted some of the central tenets of the absurd. His early resistance writing, 'Letters to a German Friend', showed how he struggled to explain his commitment to this cause as part of the will of the absurd. Pre-Second World War, the central characters in his works—Meursault, Caligula—exhibited complete indifference to morals, to the notion of good and evil. Camus would drastically change his stance in his second trilogy of works—*The Plague*, *The Just Assassins*, and *The Rebel*—which are part of Camus's cycle of revolt.

Camus develops his concept of revolt as an adaption of the absurd to the times. As he would later write in *The Rebel*, uncritically

**4. One of the most emblematic pictures of Camus, taken by famous photographer Henri Cartier-Bresson in 1947.**

following the nihilism of the absurd is not without pitfalls, for if 'nothing is right or wrong, good or bad, the rule will be about being the most efficient…and that means the strongest'. In short, the absurd does not condemn murder: 'if we pretend to accept and live the absurd outlook, we have to prepare ourselves to kill.' Revolt at first for Camus was almost instinctive—something one does in reaction to oppression but at a particular moment in time, when things have reached a certain stage where compromise or submission is no longer bearable; this stage is revolt. Revolt was the name he gave to his decision to enter the resistance, which he then turned into a theory. In September 1944, he wrote that the resistance was spurred on by revolt, not by revolution: 'revolt comes from the heart.' So, it is a feeling, like the absurd. However, it is also, like the absurd, a temporary and short-lived feeling, and does not seek to establish a system or long-standing values. Revolt is an emotion based on an inchoate moral code, a feeling that Camus first sought to illustrate in his novel *The Plague*.

# The Plague

The plot of *The Plague* is relatively simple: a city in French Algeria is overtaken by an outbreak of the plague. At the outset, the colonial order is ratified when the narrator describes the city where the events take place: 'Oran is, in fact, an ordinary city and nothing more than a French administrative district of the Algerian coast.' This description seems mundane, but what is extraordinary here is that a city in North Africa is considered the head of a French district, and that this city is described as ordinary. With that word, history is immediately ironed out: the conquest is normalized and accepted.

*The Plague* begins with an epigraph from Daniel Defoe (although it is often absent from English translations): 'It is as reasonable to represent one kind of imprisonment by another, as it is to represent anything that really exists by that which exists not.' This statement clearly sets forth the novel's allegorical objective: it is about the German occupation of France, the plague in lieu of the Germans. But, with this allegory, Camus negates human agency from history; German occupation is replaced with a virus. Throughout the novel there is no discussion of the causes of the plague; it just appears and disappears with no explanation. It is problematic as an allegory—perhaps the plague is primarily a symbol, a device to stage human beings (exclusively men) in the face of adversity and to illustrate Camus's new concept of revolt.

The city is under quarantine: first rats die, then people, no one can enter or leave. The authorities and doctors are helpless and overwhelmed. The narrative focuses on the action of six Frenchmen—Bernard Rieux, Father Paneloux, Raymond Rambert, Jean Tarrou, Joseph Grand, and Cottard, whose lives change in the face of the epidemic. Each of these six men is a stand-in for the two attitudes towards German occupation: resistance or collaboration. The characters struggle with meaning in face of the plague: what is it about, why does it exist, will they die next, what can be done about it? Facing this heightened uncertainty (after all, these are the existential problems, and made omnipresent by the plague), each of the men faces this struggle differently.

One of the main characters is Rieux, the town doctor who tirelessly takes care of patients suffering from the plague. Rieux is separated from his wife because of quarantine due to the plague—a parallel with Camus, who was separated from Francine. Though Rieux's work is ceaseless it does not produce predictable results: some of his patients die, others do not, with no explanation. Nonetheless, in the face of the arbitrariness of life he persists on moral instinct. He is pragmatic and does not dwell on the drama of the situation.

Rieux is also a crucial character because we learn toward the end of the novel that he is the narrator of the story—a plot twist that strains credulity (Rieux has been the narrator all along, reading excerpts from Tarrou's diary). Until then, the reader had been led to believe that the narrator was omniscient. Although implausible, this twist fits well with Camus's goal of challenging all god-like authorities in the novel. By telling the reader that the narrator was Rieux, Camus makes a statement about the omniscient narrator: the novel's equivalent of an all-knowing deity whom he replaces with a human character.

Asked by one of the characters if he believes in God, Rieux responds that if he believed in an all-powerful god he would stop trying to cure his patients. It is therefore not the existence of god that is challenged, but rather god's ability to intervene in human affairs. What matters is human agency. Rieux also says he cannot believe in a god that allows the death of innocent children. This exchange is at the heart of the humanist thrust of the novel.

In *The Plague* Rieux, who keeps on tending to his patients with no hope of curing them, resembles Sisyphus; it is 'an interminable defeat'. Facing death and the meaninglessness of life on a daily basis, Rieux becomes the incarnation of the man in revolt. He continues to fight for his fellow human beings no matter how dire the circumstances or elusive the chance of success. Rieux is motivated by a secular faith in humanity, which later Camus will theorize as the driving force of his revolt.

Another one of the six men is Father Paneloux, a Jesuit priest who starts out with absolute beliefs and is a stand-in for organized religion. He tells his parishioners that the plague is divine punishment—'you deserved it!'—and attacks 'vain human science'. Eventually, through his experiences with the plague, Father Paneloux becomes less intransigent, and in a particularly ironic twist dies, the plague forcibly converting him to the realm of simple mortals.

The good character who shares commonalities with Camus is Raymond Rambert, a journalist from mainland France who has come to the colonial town to inquire about the living conditions of Arabs. Rambert, trapped there because of the quarantine, tries desperately to escape for much of the novel. More concerned about reconnecting with his wife and escaping Oran for Paris, he eventually decides to stay and join the fight against the plague. He is the stand-in for the latecomer to the resistance. The initial motivation for his presence is important in that it is swiftly forgotten as soon as the plague emerges.

Jean Tarrou is another stand-in for the resister. He creates a group of volunteers and serves as the embodiment of the resistance and of revolt. Motivated by a humanist ethic, he is the most moral of the six men. Tarrou is selfless and courageous. He too dies of the plague, which further drives home the sense of meaninglessness and injustice that pervades the novel. There is no reward for good actions, whether you are an atheist man in revolt or a Jesuit priest—there is no higher benevolent authority.

A fifth man, Joseph Grand, a municipal employee who has been writing the first sentence of his novel over and over again in an attempt to reach literary perfection, eventually joins the resistance and survives the plague, once again echoing Camus's point in *The Myth of Sisyphus* about the randomness of life and death. Here the plague plays the role of Caligula (wantonly administering death), but the focus of the story is not on the source of arbitrary death but rather on how a select few human beings respond to it.

All the characters correspond to various reactions during the occupation. After the heroes (Rieux, Tarrou, Raymond, Grand), and the religious authority figure (Paneloux), we have lastly in Cottard the stand-in for the collaborator. Cottard is a man who tried to commit suicide and was saved by Grand. Cottard goes on to profit from the plague (selling goods on the black market, helping people to leave through illegal channels). He survives but will be arrested at the end of the novel. Here, human justice prevails in the absence of divine retribution.

The few times Camus mentions Algerians in the novel, it is to make them a seamless or invisible part of the decor. There are no Arab characters as such; none speak or are described, even though Oran had a substantial Algerian population.

In the end there is no explanation for the plague, how it arrived, or why it stopped killing. In fact, it just vanishes, inexplicably, ready to return at any time, as the narrator ominously warns. *The Plague* contains many of the themes found in *The Myth of Sisyphus*, along with a call for action based on moralism and humanism. As Camus wrote in his diary:

> [T]here is no other objection to the totalitarian attitude than the religious or moral objection. If this world is meaningless then they are right. I do not accept that they are right. Therefore...it is on us to create God. He is not the creator. That is all of Christianity's

history. Because we have only one way to create God and that is to become God.

To become God is what Camus suggests in this diary entry, and that is what Doctor Rieux does, in two ways: (1) by acting like a benevolent agent in times of crisis; and (2) by symbolically taking over the function of omniscient narrator. This idea of humans acting like gods would re-emerge during the course of Camus's many public arguments with communist intellectuals who derogatively called him a secular saint. Amidst all the existential questions on the existence of God and the meaning of life, a spectre intermittently haunts the novel. Though the living conditions of Arabs would be the subject of a series of articles from the novel's French journalist Rambert, this concern disappears in light of the arising emergency: the invasion of the town by the plague. The message seems to be that ordinary matters such as the 'living conditions of the Arabs' must be put to one side. Silence on this issue echoes the silence about the cause of the plague in the novel.

## *Neither Victims nor Executioners*: revolt as a political stance

In a famous series of articles written in 1947, known collectively as *Neither Victims nor Executioners*, Camus began to articulate his political vision on revolt in the post-Second World War landscape. One of his main targets in these articles was communism. The context for Camus's positioning is important: right after the Second World War the USSR was at its height in terms of influence and perceived military power. The French Communist Party was immensely powerful, in terms not just of numbers of parliament members (it was France's largest political party), but also of their union, the CGT, which was the most powerful in France.

On another front, a great many intellectuals supported the Communist Party, including artists such as Pablo Picasso and

Fernand Léger and numerous writers who congregated around the ex-surrealist Louis Aragon and the influential Communist Party literary journal *Les Lettres françaises*. As Camus knew, many communists—Lenin first among them—made the liberation and independence of former colonies a crucial objective of communism worldwide. In fact, many pro-independence movements were led by communists, starting first with Ho Chi Minh in French-occupied Indochina, a fact of which Camus was also aware. Camus's main concern at the time was that France retain its empire. For example, in an interview with a Protestant publication in 1945, Camus stated:

> If France is still treated with respect, it is not because of its glorious past. The world today does not care about glorious pasts. But it is because France is an Arab Power, a reality that 99% of French people ignore. If France does not imagine, in the years that come, a great Arab policy, there is no future for her.

The most popular analysis of colonialism at the time had at its heart the capitalist profit motive, and it was best opposed by communism, a position theorized by none other than Jean-Paul Sartre himself in a preface to an anthology of poetry from colonized authors. This stance encouraged Camus down the path of anti-communism. Camus was a man of the left, but ultimately of a European and reformist left. The distinctive features of Camus's own brand of leftism—of Euro-centrism and rejection of revolution in favour of reform—correspond to his notion of revolt. Camus's revolt was circumscribed to Europe and Europeans and framed in terms of existential issues, not social consciousness. Camus announced his specifics about revolt in *Neither Victims nor Executioners* (and further developed them in *The Rebel*).

In his first article in the series, 'The Century of Fear', Camus, in a clear attack on communism, writes against political utopia and science: 'we are suffocating amongst the men who believe to be absolutely right, whether this is about their machines or their ideas'. The question for Camus is how to get out of this terror. And the first step is to renounce all violence. The prerequisites for fighting terror are the unwillingness to be killed (to be a victim) and killing for an idea (to be an executioner). Terror here for Camus is institutionalized violence in the name of a higher cause. His target is clearly communism.

Camus writes in another article ('Socialism Mystified') that between a system where freedom prevails but not social justice, and its opposite—social justice without freedom—he would in the end choose freedom. Camus suggests strongly that the French Socialist Party—a minor entity then, but which would eventually come to power in 1981 long after Camus's death—needs to choose between complete adhesion to Marxism and the notion that the ends justify the means, or reformism. In short, Camus wants the French Socialist Party to abandon revolution and to renounce Marxism as an 'absolute philosophy'. Another reason to give up on revolution is contextual: according to Camus, the only viable revolution would be a world revolution and that would lead to a grave risk of war with a great many casualties. For Camus, this risk is not worthwhile.

Camus's alternative to world revolution is 'international democracy', a concept he only defines negatively. It is not communism, but neither is it the United Nations. Specifically, he considers the UN to be an international dictatorship because it is governed by executive powers; instead, he advocates a world parliament constituted by world elections. He notes, however, that resistance to the international dictatorship should not employ means that would contradict the desired end, a position which effectively prohibited violent resistance.

In a crucial passage of the article 'The World Goes Fast' Camus speaks of the coming 'clash of civilizations'. He claims that soon, 'in 10 years, in 50 years', it is the pre-eminence of Western civilization that will be at stake. Time is of the essence, and he asks that the world parliament he describes in the previous article be opened as soon as possible 'so that Western civilization and its world order become truly universal'. In short, Camus wants to save the pre-eminence of the West and suggests opening up a world parliament to do this. He does not say exactly how this would happen, but by advocating such a solution and by being in favour of such an objective, he resolutely places safeguarding the pre-eminence of Western powers at the centre of his agenda. This is as close as he would come to overtly defending a colonial world order.

At the end of the article, Camus advocates 'relative utopia', which would entail, for example, the nationalization of natural resources (uranium, oil, and coal) but nothing else. In short, Camus's goal is akin to the tenets of social democracy: a compromise between collectivization and all-out privatization. In his penultimate article, 'The New Social Contract', Camus wants to create an international code of justice. This is also the first article in which he proposes to outlaw the death penalty. Camus, however, is not in favour of ideological changes. He is asking men to have the courage to give up some of their dreams (i.e. communism) to focus on the saving of lives (i.e. peace). These articles are consistently lyrical and declarative in tone, as though Camus is announcing rules rather than proposing them.

The last article, despite its title 'Towards Dialogue', is no exception. Camus once again takes a stand against 'historical logic'; he describes the notion of progress, of liberation as a logic 'we created out of thin air', notions 'whose knots will end up strangling us'.

What is Camus concerned with here? The anti-historical leitmotif throughout Camus's works requires explanation. This notion of history comes from Camus's understanding of Hegel, who famously stated upon seeing Napoleon arrive in his town—and thereby toppling the aristocratic order—that he saw history on a horse. Thus, Napoleon became a personification of a progressive history. Although this is problematic in many ways (given his actions in Haiti, Spain, and elsewhere), this was the French view of Napoleon—as an emancipator of the people, a toppler of unjust regimes. The idea was that with 'progress' every oppressive regime would inexorably meet its violent end at the hands of the people.

Camus knew better than most that France had conquered Algeria and that Algerians were indeed oppressed and yearning for liberation. One way to look at Camus's anti-historicism is as the fear of a narrative that would end with the liberation of Algeria. Camus's awareness of this theory of the inevitability of progress—and on one level his belief in it—made him uneasy with the situation in Algeria. This was the source of Camus's overt appeal to his readers to relinquish their ideals, their utopia of complete liberation, in favour of a more modest 'change of lifestyle' or 'relative utopia'. Camus wanted moderate reforms, not radical change—all the more so when it came to Algeria. Though this reformist stance found few allies during the Algerian War of Independence as neither party was favouring compromise, it eventually led to renewed popularity after the fall of the Berlin Wall in 1989 and the fall of the Soviet Union; then, Camus was celebrated as having been right all along.

## The Just Assassins and The Rebel

Camus's opposition to political violence, or in his own words the condemnation of 'the right to kill in the name of history', was a vehicle for both his rejection of sweeping revolutionary change and his opposition to anti-colonialist movements. Therefore, the question of violence for a good cause, whether murder is ever justified, is at the centre of Camus's second most famous play, *The Just Assassins*, published in 1949. Basing it on the memoirs of a former Russian terrorist, Boris Savinkov, who in 1905 attempted to kill the tsar, Camus stages the dilemma of political violence through the debate among militants of a terrorist cell who are planning the assassination of the tsar.

Albert Camus

The three main characters in the play are Ivan Kaliayev, Stepan Fedorov, and Dora Doulebov. At first, the characters seem to have a seemingly unshakeable faith in the legitimacy of their actions. On the one hand, Camus presents Kaliayev as the true hero, who has scruples. Initially, he could not throw the bomb because the young nephew and niece of the tsar were present. After a second attempt, he manages to kill the Grand Duke alone. He is caught, and when authorities offer him a pardon if he betrays his comrades, he refuses. He is executed by the state in the final act. Kaliayev is the hero of the play because his actions correspond to the precise circumstances that make violence permissible according to Camus: he was willing to risk his life. Camus proposes that this willingness is a guarantee that the violence will not take place on a large scale, will be limited in time, and thus will not lead to a tyrannical regime.

Stepan, on the other hand, seems a caricature: he enthusiastically endorses the killing of innocents. He is a stand-in for the communist militant whom Camus dislikes so much, he is in favour of collective punishment, even mass murder. He is violent, intolerant, and eager to kill. For him the ends justify the means. Yet he is also fragile; he ultimately admits he was envious of Kaliayev. Dora, though a militant as well, is driven by her love for Kaliayev. Once he dies, she decides to pursue the struggle so that she may meet him in death.

The play was not well received; critics found it odd that a love story was inserted in such a political play. However, perhaps this was one of Camus's points; in the end, love seems to transcend political commitments, putting human feelings above human history, above political actions.

Although the terrorists appear flawed, Camus seems to admire them if only because they are prepared to die for their ideas as well as to kill for them. Camus contrasts this stance with that of philosophers and thinkers when he writes about 'two races of men. One kills once and pays the price of his life. The other justifies thousands of crimes and accepts all sorts of honors.' Camus's anti-intellectualism resurfaces here; he is in favour of action, even violent action, but only in the short term: the death of the violent actor is the best guarantee of the limited scope of the revolt.

The play is inseparable from Camus's later essay on revolt, *The Rebel*, because it is the transposition of an essay that Camus published before *The Just Assassins* and that he would re-insert later in *The Rebel*. This long essay is a continuation of Camus's multi-pronged attack on communism and revolution. It is for revolt what his *Myth of Sisyphus* was for the absurd: a blueprint.

Camus begins *The Rebel* by reassessing the absurd. It is recast as a starting point for revolt. Camus states that he believes in nothing, that everything is absurd, but that belief is in itself a revolt, a protest. Revolt is born out of the absurd, out of a lack of meaning; it is a reaction to the absurdity of life. Further at issue with the absurd is that it has no moral component (murder is permissible), and revolt is a reaction to this as well. For Camus, revolt is a breaking point, an existential reaction akin to someone saying, I can't go on like this! In one of the first examples Camus uses an uncharacteristic social component: the moment when a slave says 'Enough!' However, he does not address what happens next: Camusian revolt prescribes limited violence that is temporary, unsystematic, tied only to the moment.

Notwithstanding the example of the slave, a crucial point is that revolt is limited to Europe: 'the problem of revolt only has meaning inside our own Western society'. Camus adds that 'it is hard for revolt to express itself in societies with very significant inequalities'. Camus also writes that revolt cannot happen in societies where the sacred takes on great importance; in his view these societies have not yet come to terms with the absurd. Certainly, expression of the divide between Europe and the rest of the world echoes his thought on the upcoming 'clash of

civilizations' which concerns him and which he wrote about in
*Neither Victims nor Executioners*.

The paradox of *The Rebel* is that most of its many pages describe
what revolt is not. *The Rebel* includes a long list of counter-
examples—of enemies of all kinds in all fields: political (Nazis and
communists), historical (revolution), and philosophical (Hegel).

For example, Camus takes on the Marquis de Sade (the famous
French author whose pornographic stories and actions gave rise
to the word sadism and who was famously imprisoned in the
Bastille) because he was too driven by 'absolute hatred' of his
fellow man. Camus criticizes Romantic writers because their
revolt is limited, too literary, and individualist. He discusses
Dostoyevsky's *Brothers Karamazov* but sees it as offering a dead
end because Karamazov's refusal of God's truth leads him to
madness in which 'everything is permitted'—harking back to the
nihilism associated with the absurd.

Camus also discusses human revolt as art, as an artistic expression,
and here he sees revolt as existential, not social. As the book
progresses, its tone becomes more virulent. Camus issues edicts
on human nature and on what we should and should not believe.
He brandishes an undefined humanistic moral against any and
all large-scale emancipating projects. Any dissent from Camus's
point of view becomes a voice in favour of mass murder and
'servitude'. His statements are definitive and bear no discussion.

The paradox is that, for example, when Camus restricts to
Europeans those issues pertaining to human nature and revolt, he
leaves himself open to the criticism that he himself is the
messianic teller of truths which he criticizes so thoroughly elsewhere
in the essay.

The essay concludes with a curiously regionalist note praising
'Mediterranean thought', which for Camus is synonymous with

certain distinct intellectual attributes, which include a particular sensitivity to nature and a privileged relationship with the sun. Certainly, Camus was grateful for being born in that area of the world and not in the working-class cities of mainland France:

> What good luck to have been born to the world on the hills of Tipasa instead of in Saint-Étienne or Roubaix. Know my luck and receive it with gratitude.

This section received a fair amount of criticism. Can a particular thought and world outlook be linked to geography, to weather patterns, as Camus seemed to say? At the time, many critics were not convinced.

The intransigent tone, the exclusion of non-Europeans from revolt, and the equation of Nazism with communism led many intellectuals from all sides to criticize the book virulently when it was published. Though initially he did not want to, Camus's long-time friend Jean-Paul Sartre would become the strongest and most persuasive critic of *The Rebel*. This launched the very public break between France's two most famous intellectuals at the time.

# Chapter 5
# Camus and Sartre—the breaks that made them inseparable

When Camus's *The Stranger* and *The Myth of Sisyphus* were published in 1942, Jean-Paul Sartre was already an established author. But Camus and Sartre had not yet met. Part of Sartre's claim to fame arose from the 1938 publication of his first novel, *Nausea*, in which a teacher in a provincial city experiences intense moments of existential doubt upon staring at the roots of a tree. It was a novel that took literary Paris by storm. *The Stranger* is similar to *Nausea* in many ways, telling the story of a disaffected, solitary man who questions everything around him—society and the meaning of life. They are also, however, two different novels: in *Nausea* nature provokes the existential angst, but art—in the form of jazz—resolves it (or gives hope), while in *The Stranger* nature soothes Meursault's angst, and art is absent.

In 1938 and 1939 Camus reviewed *Nausea* and Sartre's subsequent collection of short stories (*The Wall*). The reviews were a mix of obligatory praise and subtle put-downs. Camus wrote that he liked half of the novel, but not the part he deemed to be lectures on philosophy. He praised the creative aspects of the novel but did not appreciate the philosophical reflections; the combination of the two made it impossible for Camus to consider *Nausea* as a novel, or as a work of art of any kind. Further, Camus found Sartre's belief in the power of art to offer hope of a meaning for life almost laughable. For Camus nothing could transcend the absurdity of life. The concluding paragraph of his first review ended on a somewhat contradictory high note. Camus praised Sartre's 'limitless talent', stating he eagerly looked forward to future works and adding—ironically—to Sartre's lessons as well. Clearly, Camus resented the professor in Sartre.

When Sartre reviewed *The Stranger* four years later it was from a position of strength—as Sartre was the accomplished author. Sartre's status also derived from his prestigious scholarly *parcours* or itinerary: Sartre, alongside Simone de Beauvoir, his lifelong companion, was a member of the elite École Normale Supérieure. This is in contrast with Camus. It is understandable that Camus's resentment toward the French educational system would project itself onto Sartre, one of its brightest stars.

It is thus ironic that when Sartre reviewed Camus's *The Stranger* and *The Myth of Sisyphus* in February 1943, his critique reads very much like a detailed report or a lesson, down to the title: 'Explanation of *The Stranger*'. Indeed, it is on the subject of philosophy that Sartre was his harshest with Camus. A couple of pages into the review, Sartre admonished Camus about his writing in *The Myth of Sisyphus* as though he were a student, an inadequate one at that: 'Camus wants to please by quoting texts by Jaspers, by Heidegger, by Kierkegaard, which it seems he does not always understand.' (This criticism was later echoed by de Beauvoir, who wrote in her memoirs that Camus 'perused books, but did not read them'.) Sartre continued in this vein by saying that Camus 'chitchats' in *The Myth of Sisyphus* despite professing 'his love of silence'. Camus did not really consider *Nausea* to be a genuine novel, and in turn Sartre was dubious about whether *The Stranger* merited the term. He concluded that Camus did not succeed in achieving his goal.

These assessments of Camus came from a reviewer who at that time outranked him in philosophical knowledge and literary prestige. How did Camus react? He complained to his mentor

Jean Grenier about the review's 'acid tone' but also candidly acknowledged Sartre's intellectual might: 'on many occasions it helps me understand what I was trying to do'. These last few words are quite the statement: Camus virtually admits that Sartre could understand his own works better than he did.

When the two writers first met, in occupied Paris a few months after Sartre's review, they became fast friends: often getting together in cafés (see Figure 5)—one of the few places that had heating under Nazi occupation—talking, drinking, and joking. Sartre particularly liked Camus for what Beauvoir described in her memoirs as his 'ruffian ways'—a contrast to his careful prose. Camus was not as sophisticated as his new Parisian friends: for example, when in the street or in a café, upon sighting a woman he thought attractive Camus would immediately interrupt the conversation, stop talking or listening, and ostentatiously stare at the object of his attention. A decade later, Clamence, the main character in his novel *The Fall*, would declare that he would rather chat with an attractive woman than have a conversation with Einstein. Camus wanted to be perceived as a Don Juan, and indeed he acted like one: he had many, often overlapping, affairs during his lifetime.

Thus, in those early days of friendship, Camus was a person whose company Sartre enjoyed; they mostly socialized and there were no long conversations about one another's works. In 1943 many renowned writers from the French publisher Gallimard and prominent artists would go to parties together, most famously one in Picasso's home, where they all participated in his play.

Toward the end of the occupation, Camus asked Sartre to join him at *Combat* as a reporter. After joining the staff, Sartre wrote many articles on the skirmishes and barricades that took place during the liberation of Paris; he also travelled to New York as part of a US-sponsored invitation of French journalists to strengthen the ties between the two Allied countries. At this stage, Sartre had

5. **Jean-Paul Sartre and Simone de Beauvoir.**

given his immensely popular lecture on existentialism and it was published one year later. Existentialism was extremely fashionable at the time and Sartre and de Beauvoir were clearly at the forefront of this philosophical phenomenon.

One thing was clear: Camus did not want people to think he was a disciple of Sartre and took pains to explain he was not an existentialist. However, few people made the distinction between Camus's absurd and Sartre's existentialism: Camus was often described as an existentialist (and he still is), and this label irritated him to the extent that he would often put pen to paper to reject the affiliation, sometimes playfully but occasionally forcefully.

When a well-respected critic wrote that 'all of Camus' *Caligula* was merely an illustration of the existentialist principles of Mr. Sartre', Camus replied: 'I am beginning to become a little (only a little) irritated by the continual confusion that involves me with existentialism.' This was an understatement. His response comprised three bulleted points in which he pointed out (1) that Caligula was written in 1938, before the rise of Sartre's existentialism, (2) that *The Myth of Sisyphus* was written against existentialism, and (3) that ultimately, he did not have enough trust in reason to belong to a system of thought. Despite this clarification, confusion remained, and the questions kept coming.

During his own voyage to New York City in June 1946, to the same questions posed by an American journalist Camus responded in a more playful manner, but not without irony:

> No, I am not an existentialist. Sartre and I are always surprised to find our two names joined together. We are contemplating publishing an ad where the undersigned will affirm having nothing in common...

The differences between existentialism and Camus's absurd were clear from the start: existentialism is human-centred, about personal responsibility in a collective world, whereas the absurd is a divorce from human affairs and, ostensibly, a rejection of all systems.

It was precisely this point of divergence between the absurd and existentialism that led to the writers' first genuine row. The context was the very early days of the Cold War pitting the USA against the USSR, and it was virtually impossible not to choose sides. Camus was almost by definition anti-communist. Even back when he was a Communist Party member, it was clear from his jokes with his mentor that he was no communist. (Recall that Camus's reason to be in the party was not to adhere to the communist doctrine, but rather to try to prevent Arab resisters to France's presence in Algeria from starting a party of their own.)

One evening in 1946, at a party hosted by writer, musician, and singer Boris Vian, Camus had a huge row with Maurice Merleau-Ponty, a philosopher close to Sartre who had just written an article which stated that one had to take sides in the great conflicts of one's time, that there was no alternative. Refusing to do so was siding with the oppressor: one had to be involved in human affairs. This was a lesson of the resistance as it applied to the Cold War and Merleau-Ponty advocated being on the side of the USSR. This infuriated Camus, who equated this position with an unconditional support of Stalin (and, on another level, with the obligation to commit to a cause, any cause); he vehemently argued with Merleau-Ponty and then stormed out of the apartment. Sartre and another friend unsuccessfully tried to get him to rejoin the party, but Camus refused.

Merleau-Ponty's position was anathema for Camus, who hated the idea of having to take sides, forced as it were by historical events. Camus was angry at the Germans for 'forcing him into History' and would rather move from one cause to another, without any permanent commitment. Though he supported great principles and ideas, he never openly adhered to a cause or an ideology—least of all communism because it had been historically linked with the struggle against colonialism. And, the connection between communism and anti-colonial struggle had become more prevalent in the aftermath of the Second World War.

For Camus the colonial issue was complicated: it could not boil down to simple approval or disapproval. While he was aware of and condemned injustices towards Arabs, French Algeria was his birthplace, home to all his family and many of his friends, and he was devoted to it.

After this break, Camus and Sartre did not speak until the following year, and then only upon a chance encounter. When seeing one another socially they got along well, but Camus would say that as soon as he was away from Sartre he liked him less.

Shortly after the row, Sartre published an unsigned editorial in *Les Temps modernes* titled 'Both Executioners and Victims'. (*Les Temps modernes* had been founded in October 1945 by Sartre after *La Nouvelle Revue française* was shut down because of its collaboration with German authorities during the occupation.) This editorial was Sartre's first public reaction to France's colonial war in Indochina and served as a direct rebuttal to Camus's pacifist series of articles *Neither Victims nor Executioners*. In it, Sartre broke with all parliamentary parties, condemned the war, and called for the withdrawal of French troops from Indochina. Sartre's editorial justified revolutionary violence and compared France's presence in Indochina to the German occupation, provoking the outrage of many commentators—and no doubt Camus's ire. Seven years later, in 1954, on the day of a catastrophic French military defeat in Indochina which eventually led to France's withdrawal from the region, Camus wrote in his diary:

> 8 May, 1954. Fall of Dien Bien Phu. As in [19]40, mixed feeling of shame and anger. At the eve of the massacre, the result is clear. Right-wing politicians put poor souls in an impossible situation and at the same time, the men of the left shot them in the back.

Comparing the Indochinese to the Germans was precisely contrary to Sartre's position. It became clear that on the issue of colonialism Sartre and Camus were in opposite camps.

The two men had another ongoing disagreement with respect to the question of political violence. In 1946 Camus had published a short piece—*Les Meurtriers délicats*—discussing Russian terrorists who tried to kill members of the tsar's family at various periods from the late 19th to the early 20th century. The dilemmas and actions of those terrorist groups were of critical importance for Camus. Was it right to kill a member of the tsar's family? What about their children? Was murder ever justified? These questions would be at the heart of Camus's play *The Just Assassins*.

For Sartre these issues were *passé*, at best a distraction. In his play *Dirty Hands* Sartre subtly expressed his view of Camus's interest in Russian terrorists. Two party leaders, Louis and Hugo, discuss political actions:

HUGO:  In Russia at the end of the last century, there were guys who put bombs in their pockets and stood in the path of a Grand Duke. The bomb exploded, the Grand Duke died and the fellow as well. I can do that.

LOUIS:  Those were Anarchists. You are dreaming of this because you are like them: an intellectual anarchist. You are fifty years behind the times: terrorism is over.

HUGO:  So I am an incompetent.

LOUIS:  In this area, yes.

Sartre parodied Camus's interest and belittled Hugo, the character voicing his ideas. But this literary sniping was indirect—almost an aside.

However, the publication of Camus's *The Rebel* made a full-scale confrontation inevitable. In this long essay, Camus compared communism to Nazism and asserted that it led invariably to oppression and wholesale murder. In the context of the Cold War, this was a line drawn in the sand. And by the standards of those times, this meant siding with the USA.

Sartre looked at things more pragmatically. Although he condemned Stalinism, and later the USSR (over the 1956 invasion of Hungary), he supported the Communist Party during the latter part of the war in Algeria. He was also an early and ardent supporter of the Cuban revolution but withdrew his support when the Cuban government jailed dissident poet Herberto Padilla. Sartre was shocked when *The Rebel* came out in 1952 and did not want to review Camus's book because of their friendship, such as it was. Instead, Francis Jeanson, a French philosopher close to Sartre (and who would later become an active supporter of the pro-independence Algerian National Liberation Front), wrote the review. He had no affinities with Camus and had been critical of him in the past.

The review was scathing: Jeanson first noted that the book was well reviewed by the left and by the right and rhetorically wondered if this was because the work and its ideas were malleable, 'capable of assuming diverse forms'. He took Camus to task for his 'vague humanism' and ended by pointing out that Camus focused in his book almost exclusively on the victims of Stalinism. What about the victims from Western regimes, what about the colonized but also European workers, what about the 'miner, the state employee punished for going on strike…', the Vietnamese 'cleansed' by napalm, the Tunisians 'picked up' by the Foreign Legion? It was a conclusion that pushed Camus on a topic he did not want to discuss.

Camus was incensed. He wrote a response in *Les Temps modernes*, but not to Jeanson; instead he chose to address Sartre as the publisher, implying that Sartre had written the review, or at the very least that he bore the responsibility for allowing it to be published. In his response, Camus refused to discuss Jeanson's points directly, doubled down on his critique of Stalinism, and asked why Jeanson/Sartre had not condemned Stalin's 'concentration camps', challenging them to do so. He wrote that unless they addressed his request for unequivocal condemnation, further dialogue was impossible. He also condemned the tone of Jeanson's review and later complained in his diary: 'Polemic with T.M. [*Les Temps*

*modernes*].... Paris is a jungle, and its wild beasts are miserable.'
He complained variously about 'insult[s], the denunciation of
their brother'. Ultimately, his response dodged the colonial
question posed by Jeanson and was a counter-punch on the issue
of the USSR.

Sartre was pitiless in his reply, amplifying the old put-downs of
his first review of *The Stranger* written ten years earlier. Writing
with great verve, he wondered if *The Rebel* was not proof of
Camus's incompetence as a philosopher; he called him out for
'hating intellectual efforts' and for his habit of not reading
primary sources. Sartre reminded Camus how he had criticized
Stalinism and cited editorials in *Les Temps modernes*
condemning the USSR as proof. Sartre also highlighted the use
of condemnations of the USSR by the mainstream press as a
means to minimize the plight of the colonized, echoing and
amplifying Jeanson's conclusion. Sartre stated that he could
criticize both the West and the East, and he rhetorically asked
Camus, why can't you? Sartre then pointed out Camus's
ambiguous position on Indochina and concluded by simultaneously
offering to publish Camus's eventual response and announcing
that, for his part, the exchange was over.

That second break was the end of their odd friendship. They
would never speak again. Yet they continued to communicate
indirectly via their works, throughout their lives. After their public
break, the critique of the bourgeois left-wing intellectual was a
mainstay in Camus's written works, as were attacks on Sartre and
existentialism in his diary.

As a result of the very public exchange of letters about *The Rebel*,
Sartre was widely considered the victor, having outwritten
and outwitted Camus, who was left isolated. Camus even
contemplated—in true macho *pied-noir* fashion—beating up
Sartre but lamented that Sartre was too small. He avoided the
Latin Quarter and the cafés where Sartre and de Beauvoir

congregated with friends, and generally shut himself off from society. Although he also stopped publicly engaging with the controversy, he addressed all the critiques in an extensive response, titled 'Defense of *The Rebel*', which was not published during his lifetime.

## The Fall

The work that gave the most space to Camus's dispute not just with Sartre but with his contemporaries was *The Fall*. It is the tale of a solitary man named Clamence, a former lawyer who lived in France but is in self-imposed exile in Amsterdam. In a run-down bar, called Mexico-City, he talks non-stop to another Frenchman, who remains anonymous until the very last pages, where it is disclosed that he too is a lawyer. Here's how they meet:

> May I, Sir, offer you my services without bothering you? I am afraid you may be unable to communicate with the respectable Gorilla that presides over the destinies of this establishment. Indeed, he only speaks Dutch. Unless you authorize me to plead your case, he will not know that you would like some Jenever. There, I dare hope he understood me: this nod must signify that he has given in to my entreaties.

The two men meet five times, and in each encounter Clamence (a combination of Camus's name and the French word for clemency) goes on and on: digressions, jokes, anecdotes, musing, general statements about France, the world, women, politics, religion…

Clamence calls himself a 'penitent judge' who specializes in noble causes. Penitent judges (as defined in the novel) feel guilty because of their social background and their privilege and thus embrace the cause of the disenfranchised as a form of penance, but they become so involved in their role that they stand in judgement of others. (In a diary entry Camus wrote that penitent judges are existentialists.)

Clamence describes himself as a defender of the widow and her fatherless son and explains that his legal practice focused on helping the oppressed, the poor, the wronged. Yet by Clamence's own admission his compassion is self-serving. He confesses that he rushes to the aid of a blind man solely to feel the satisfaction of having helped him. Helping others for Clamence is a demonstration of his narcissism, not of genuine generosity. Behind selflessness lies vanity: for example, Clamence refuses the highest French civilian decorations because his refusal is more gratifying than acceptance of the medal.

Each page of *The Fall* finds Clamence musing on a variety of topics. There is even a dig at France, in which he says nastiness is a national pastime. In this sea of 'anecdotes and fanciful commentary', an event stands out. Walking through Paris one night, Clamence hears the scream of a woman who threw herself in the Seine. This is 'the fall'. Yet, despite his public persona, his ostensibly humanitarian outlook, Clamence walks away from the scene without helping the woman. Presumably she dies. Two or three years later, while on a cruise, he sees a black spot on the ocean and immediately thinks of the woman; he realizes he has to face his guilt and drop the pretence of humanism—he must be himself. (Certain commentators likened this to Camus's contradictions with Algeria, since he famously stopped writing about it publicly after 1954; rather than face an intractable problem, Camus symbolically walked away from it.)

Yet the scene where Clamence ignores a woman throwing herself into the river could also be construed as an attack on Sartre, who from Camus's perspective spoke of helping others but did not concretely help them. In fact, according to some critics, this quote may correspond to Camus's conception of communism as a secular religion in *The Rebel*: 'And every time I can, I preach in my church of Mexico-City, I invite the good people to submit to authority and humbly to solicit the comforts of slavery, even if I have to present it as true freedom.' Clamence continues: 'I learned at least that I was on the side of the guilty, of the accused only to the precise extent to which their fault would cause me no harm. Their guilt made me eloquent because I was not the victim of it.'

Clamence concludes his tirade with the reasons why he decided to end his career as a penitent judge: 'when I was threatened in turn, I did not only become a judge, but worse: an irascible master who wanted—outside the law—to knock out the delinquent and bring him to his knees. After that, my dear compatriot, it is rather difficult to seriously continue to believe one's vocation to justice and the predestined defender of widows and orphans.' This last sentence was emblematic of Camus's criticism against communism: it turned humanistic impulses into an ideology that proposed to change the world.

It would be a mistake, however, to read *The Fall* as exclusively a series of attacks on Sartre, since many aspects of Clamence have more to do with Camus himself. *The Fall* is in many ways a self-portrait. Upon finishing the draft, Camus confided to his friend and critic Roger Quillot that he was concerned about his second wife Francine's reaction upon reading the manuscript.

The scene of the fall is also similar to Francine's suicide attempt: according to Quillot she once attempted to kill herself by jumping out of a window. Camus recounted this incident in a letter to his lover, the famous French actress Maria Casarès. Many of Camus's experiences with and thoughts on women as expressed in his diary are echoed by Clamence in *The Fall*. Clamence sees himself as a prisoner of desire—other than for sexual contact, women bore him.

The numerous passages about women in *The Fall* echo Camus's glorification of Don Juan in *The Myth of Sisyphus* as an archetypal absurd man who experiences true *bonheur* going from conquest to conquest. In *The Fall*, Clamence boasts of acting different parts to get his way with women and states that 'not to take what one desires is "the most difficult thing in the world"'. In his diary

Camus considered his attraction to women an infirmity, 'a servitude'. For Clamence there is a desire to control women, even those he is no longer with. Clamence talks about asking women he no longer wants to swear fidelity to him. Camus writes to Casarès telling her that when apart from one another, he wants her locked up in a room. It is clear that there is a connection between Clamence and Camus's views on women.

Francine was suicidal, at least in part as a result of his affairs, and Quillot reports that she questioned him: 'you always denounce the weaknesses of others, but what about your own?'

Aside from his wife, Camus's views on women and on feminism (which he despised) led him to clash with the person closest to Sartre: Simone de Beauvoir, author of numerous novels and essays. De Beauvoir wrote one of the foundational feminist works: *The Second Sex*. Upon its publication, Camus expressed his dislike of the book and said it humiliated the French male. De Beauvoir in reply was as ruthless as Sartre: she said that Camus, besides his sexist reaction to *The Second Sex*, 'did not admit disagreements; if some were forthcoming, he would give in to angry outbursts that seemed like an escape'. She continued, 'he had an idea of himself that no work, nor any revelation would shake'. She also described him as lazy: 'he perused books instead of reading them'. To top it all off, her most successful novel, *Les Mandarins*, featured a problematic and troubled character, Henri Perron, who was widely interpreted to be a stand-in for Camus. The fact that her novel received the Prix Goncourt, France's most prestigious literary prize, upset him.

The tension between Camus and Sartre, as well as with de Beauvoir, continued beyond the grave. In Camus's posthumously published novel *The First Man* there were frequent passages portraying Parisian intellectuals as ignorant of the lives of the *pied-noir* working class they criticize. In this largely autobiographical novel, he viewed these intellectuals as back-stabbers, perhaps even traitors; it is clear that he despised them. It is also clear that Sartre, among others, was being targeted. A few years after Camus's death, at a conference in Japan, Sartre gave a talk on intellectuals. Contrasting authentic and inauthentic intellectuals, he wrote:

> Hiding behind certain vague and lofty universal values, these false intellectuals say: 'our colonial methods are not what they should be, there are too many inequalities in our overseas territories. But I am against all violence, wherever it comes from; I want to be neither victim nor executioner and that is why I oppose the revolt of indigenous people against colonizers.'

Sartre succinctly pointed out that 'this pseudo-universalist stance really means the following: "I am in favor of the chronic violence the colonizers inflict on the colonized (overexploitation, unemployment, malnutrition, all held in place by terror)".' This was a clear attack on Camus—and on *Neither Victims nor Executioners*.

Sartre's opposition to the French occupation of Algeria was total and uncompromising; he supported French deserters and famously wished for the French army to lose. Camus offered compromises: he first proposed a system of limited sovereignty for Algeria, then a truce, then remained silent. Importantly, however, one of the few constants in his public life was his opposition to Algerian independence. In short, colonialism was at the centre of the ongoing dispute between the two men.

# Chapter 6
# Camus and Algeria

Camus was always ambivalent about colonialism in Algeria and this ambivalence greatly affected him. In 1943, he wrote in his diary:

> Algeria. I do not know if I make myself understood well. But I have the same feeling when returning to Algeria that one does looking at the face of a child. And despite this, I know that all is not pure.

In the late 1930s Camus had advocated the passage of the Blum–Viollette bill, which would have granted French citizenship to a very small minority of Arab men (a few thousand). All efforts to pass the bill had failed in the 1930s, but the Second World War changed everything. During the German occupation, French resistance leaders, desperate for Arab support, accepted a proposal—*The Manifesto of the Algerian People*—from Arab nationalist leaders, including Messali Hadj representing the Algerian People's party (PPA), Sheikh Bachir al-Ibrahimi for the Muslim religious scholars, and Ferhat Abbas for those in favour of autonomy. The goal of the *Manifesto* was the establishment of an autonomous Algerian state.

Although in March 1943 the governor of French Algeria accepted the *Manifesto* as a basis for forthcoming negotiations, he later withdrew his support. The original granting of the *Manifesto* had raised the hopes of Algerian nationalists. This withdrawal, combined with the desperation of the Algerian people, gravely suffering from wartime food restrictions, created an explosive situation.

In early 1944, Charles de Gaulle, now head of the Provisional Government of the French Republic, the interim government of France, offered to pass the Blum–Viollette bill into law. However, sensing weakness, the Algerian nationalist leaders refused. The French authorities continued to blow hot and cold: on 7 March 1944, de Gaulle unilaterally revoked the indigenous code (though there were still no equal voting rights), but on 25 April 1945, he had Messali Hadj, the most charismatic, radical, and courageous Algerian nationalist leader, deported to Brazzaville in the Congo. This was the context for the riots of VE Day that ended with the massacres in Sétif and Guelma. An Algerian population which had suffered the wartime restrictions more than the metropolitan French, a nationalist leadership which had believed that independence was at hand, a people who had contributed thousands of its young men to the first French victories on the Italian front—were now unable to wave their own flag in celebration of VE Day. The French and *pieds-noirs'* reaction was a veritable massacre which lasted for weeks; thousands of Algerians were slaughtered. It set back for ten years the movement for Algerian independence, but it also ensured that upon its re-emergence the actors would be more determined than ever. The context for the month-long repression was a weakened French state, desperate to hold on to a colonial empire by any means.

Though he never discussed in detail the massacres of Sétif and Guelma, Camus was enthusiastic about the abolition of the indigenous code and the de facto passing of the Blum–Viollette bill, although the bloody massacres showed that it was too little, too late. Camus pushed for more rights to be granted to Algerians after the war. He wanted more Algerians to have access to education and all graduates from primary school to obtain French citizenship, yet he stopped short of asking for voting rights for all. Camus was to be the advocate of peace and compromise, with one objective in mind: for Algeria to remain French. He appealed mainly to the metropolitan authorities, writing in the press that the effort to retain Algeria as a part of France demanded a 'second conquest'; in other words, Algerian hearts and minds had to be won over.

However, the situation demanded greater concessions, a fact of which Camus was acutely aware. In the aftermath of the Second World War, it was no longer possible to ignore the demands of colonized people for their rights; these demands surfaced at every level: political, cultural, and on the streets. During this period, the long-repressed colonial reality began slowly to emerge in Camus's fiction, until it eventually took centre stage.

## The Exile and the Kingdom

*The Exile and the Kingdom*, the last of Camus' s fiction published in his lifetime, is a collection of short stories, many of which are steeped in the North African context. Some of these stories echo Camus's anger at Sartre and the aftermath of their quarrel. But in others his growing concern with the rise of nationalism in Algeria is omnipresent, though never discussed directly until 'The Host'.

The first short story, 'The Adulterous Woman', is the story of Janine, the wife of a *pied-noir* cloth salesman. They travel by bus into the desert—200 miles south of Algiers—so that he can sell his wares to the local population. Camus tells the story from her point of view—her impressions as they go deeper into what increasingly seems a foreign land. At first, Janine describes Arabs as an indistinct group. She feels they are feigning sleep; she does not like their silence and indifference. Throughout the story, she feels estranged by Arabs and comments on their language, which she heard all her life but does not understand. She hates the 'stupid arrogance' of an Arab who is looking at her, to which her husband adds, 'they think they can do anything *now*'. These remarks highlight that the abolition of the indigenous code in 1944 is a source of the *pieds-noirs*' fear. There is also fear of coming unrest. The entire time, the wife feels that all the Arabs are surrounding her, as though they are an oppressive force.

In the final scene, Janine wakes up in the middle of the night, goes onto the balcony, stares into the horizon, and is enthralled by the forces of nature—a quintessential Camusian moment of *bonheur*, a 'perfect' moment when 'time stops'. Simultaneously, the sounds from the Arab town stop. (In Camus's words: 'A knot that habit, boredom, years had tied, was coming undone, slowly.') Symbolically, the Arabs are gone. In an intense communion with nature she transcends the cold, the weight of others, the anguish of living and dying. Finally, upon returning and facing her husband in their small hotel room she is overcome with tears. She has experienced a cathartic moment.

For Camus, these symbolic moments of merger with nature represent a powerful rejection of human history. It is the fantasy of an atemporal Algeria void of most of its indigenous inhabitants, an inchoate fantasy which is the sole source of true, intense bliss—or *bonheur*—for the character, and indeed for Camus himself.

'The Host' is arguably the most powerful story in the collection. The hero is Daru, a *pied-noir* teacher. He lives in the mountains of Algeria in a home which doubles as the school. Daru is greeted one cold winter morning with the arrival on a donkey of Balducci, a tough local policeman with a heart of gold—a version of the salt of the earth *pied-noir* who appears frequently in Camus's fiction. With Balducci, on foot and tied to the donkey with a rope, is a local Arab man accused of killing a relative. (As in *The Stranger*, the Arab is never named.) Daru is summarily charged with bringing the man to the authorities, something he is loath to do. But Balducci makes it a matter of loyalty and honour to try and force Daru's hand, to put him on the spot. Camus felt the same way during the Algerian War of Independence, stuck between two warring parties with no way to express his own perspective. Thus, the hero Daru can be seen as a stand-in for Camus.

Though Daru accepts Balducci's account of the Arab man's guilt at face value, he does not want to deliver him to the authorities. Neither does he want to upset the old man. To put pressure on Daru, Balducci says that war is brewing, Arabs may rise up, and then 'we will all be involved'. Daru does not want to be involved, but historical events catch up with him. Daru and Balducci argue and finally, reluctantly, Daru agrees to sign a note confirming that he has received the prisoner, but he does not promise to deliver him. This creates a rift between the two men. Once Balducci leaves, Daru feels guilty that he let Balducci down. Daru, like Camus, is caught between the desire to avoid conflict and his allegiance and closeness to the *pied-noir* community.

Furious at the Arab for committing a murder and upset at Balducci for ordering him to deliver the prisoner to the authorities, Daru is caught between two conflicting allegiances. So, in the end Daru compromises. He brings the Arab halfway toward the city and the prison and tells him that east is prison and south are nomads who would take him as one of their own. After hesitating, the Arab goes east, and Daru returns home.

Camus portrays Daru as a man caught between two factions, but a kind man who tries to be fair. We are meant to feel empathy for him, which does not prepare us for the shock of the final paragraph. Upon returning to his classroom, Daru finds written on the blackboard the followings words of menace: 'You have delivered our brother. You will pay.' Kind, fair, but misunderstood by all, alone, pressured by his own, threatened by Arabs—this is how Camus saw himself in the midst of the struggle for Algerian independence.

Commentators are split on the interpretation of the end of the story: the focus is on either Daru as a genuinely noble figure (after all, he refuses to send the Arab man to prison), or on how odd it is for a narrative set in colonial times to have a settler portrayed as a victim and sole sympathetic character.

## A civil truce

The war in Algeria, which began on All Saints' Day in 1954, was affecting Camus not only as a writer, a French citizen, and a *pied-noir*, but also as a public figure. Two years after the start of the war, Camus travelled to Algiers to give a talk, an impassioned plea for peace. This is known as his *Call for a Civil Truce in Algeria*.

He was under no illusion about stopping the war; his objective was an agreement between the two warring parties to end the killing of innocents. The atmosphere surrounding Camus's intervention was one of hostility from unexpected quarters: the *pied-noir* mayor of Algiers had refused to host the conference, and when a venue was found—thanks to moderate Algerian organizations, who also organized security—he could hear hostile cries from the street of the *pieds-noirs* crowd: 'Death to Camus! Death to Mendès-France (premier of France, 1954–5, who had been in favour of ending colonial wars)! Long live French Algeria!' Ultimately, the conference was shortened for fear of violence from the *pieds-noirs* groups.

Camus opened his speech by immediately condemning the protesters who wished to silence him. It was a moving retelling of his motivation and his plight: 'for 20 years I have done what I could to help concord between our two people'. It was also an admission of failure: you can heckle me, you can even laugh at me, Camus implied, but at this stage the emergency is to prevent undue suffering.

He attempted to separate the Algerians' fight for justice from their fight for independence, which he described as 'foreign ambitions' which would definitively ruin France. Was this a reference to the Soviet Union? In the Cold War context, the spectre of the Soviet Union taking over was a classic argument which supporters of colonial powers made for continued control over a colony. At the heart of the speech was this: for Camus, Algerian nationalism could not be allowed to express itself formally at the expense of France; Algerian independence was out of the question. Keep at it, and there will be perpetual war, Camus said to his largely Algerian audience. His message of peace also included an indirect warning: if you don't negotiate, the fighting will continue ad infinitum.

Camus concluded by praising the members of the Muslim community for organizing the conference and told the mixed audience that what moved them was humanism, not politics. Camus here displayed an almost endearing naivety; in fact, the Algerian National Liberation Front (FLN) was the force behind the conference. Amar Ouzegane, a friend of Camus and a fellow member of the Communist Party in the 1930s, was one of the organizers of the conference. He was also, unbeknownst to Camus, a member of the FLN. The objective was to claim Camus, to convince him that the revolution was justified.

Many years later Ouzegane would explain: 'the civil truce was a way for us [the FLN] to help honest folks, enemies of injustice but hostile to violence, to open their eyes and to progressively realize that the FLN was right'. Did the FLN have a chance to convince Camus? This was very unlikely, but certainly that Camus gave his speech for peace surrounded by hundreds of *pieds-noirs* baying for his death was a step in the right direction as far as the FLN was concerned; for them, it was a public relations coup.

This moment is emblematic of Camus's ambiguous position arising from the combination of his sincere desire for peace and his inability to perceive the scope of the injustice suffered by

Algerians throughout the French occupation. Camus oscillates between nationalism and humanism, desperately attempting the impossible combination of the two.

In a letter to a close friend after the conference, Camus writes, 'I returned from Algeria quite depressed. What is happening is strengthening my conviction. It is all for me a "*malheur personnel*".' As *malheur* in French is the opposite of *bonheur*, for Camus this was a tragedy, and a personal disaster (Figure 6).

Throughout his life, Camus repressed his modest *pied-noir* origins in various ways: by the style of his dress starting as a teenager, by the style and subject matter of his first three major works (universal themes), even by his focus on Spain, the country which outwardly most concerned him from a political perspective (rather

6. **Camus, anguished.**

than Algeria), and which served as an idealized space where he could combine his Spanish roots with a progressive cause. But, in the late 1950s, with the very existence of French Algeria at stake, Camus had no choice but to address his roots and takes sides in the ongoing conflict, as he would in his posthumous novel *The First Man*. It is perhaps for that reason the best introduction to his work, for it makes clear what is at the root of his refusal of history and what motivates his veneration of nature.

What emerges in his fiction but was until then always implicit or hidden is an unvarnished emotional defence of French settlers, of French Algeria—it is a coming out, a mask that falls: nothing is more important to Camus than France's presence in Algeria. This is the story of the hidden genesis behind his works, his commitments, his worldview, even his love of nature. His last book, *The First Man*, is the sincere cry of a man who feels he has nothing to lose, nothing to hide any more. It is the key to all his works.

This unfinished novel takes place mostly during the war. There is a clear sense that Algerians are going to reclaim their country, and pervasive feelings of anxiety, fear, and anger on the part of the settlers at the centre of the story. Camus tries to justify the French presence in Algeria: he is facing the colonial situation from an unprecedented position, from a place of weakness. The war is Camus's worst fear come true. The novel itself is highly autobiographical; it is the story of a *pied-noir* named Jacques Cormery, who now lives in France. (In the manuscript he occasionally is named Albert and Cormery was Camus's paternal grandmother's last name.) A first-person narrative from Jacques alternates with dialogues between settlers and Jacques's childhood memories. When Jacques, who lives in Paris, returns to his native land, he is confronted with the settlers' anger, fear, and resentment towards the rise of Arab nationalism. The novel features lengthy dialogues between an aggrieved settler and a less intransigently anti-Arab one alongside a narrator who attempts to make us understand the settlers' anger.

One such dialogue occurs when Levesque, a friend of Jacques's father, reminisces about their 1905 service in the French army fighting Moroccans. Upon finding the mutilated body of a French soldier—which is described at length—Jacques's father says about Moroccan combatants:

> 'A man stops himself. That's what a man does, if not…' And then he calmed down.…And suddenly he shouted: 'Filthy race, what a race, all of them, all…'

This passage is in keeping with many others in the novel, where most of the dialogue denies the humanity of Arabs. The actions of Arabs against the French invaders are described in detail, while the crimes of Europeans are only suggested. The end of this passage is also emblematic, for it concludes with a definitive judgement about race emanating from the father figure, who is idealized throughout the novel. His racist cry is presented to the reader as the 'understandable' reaction of a victim. Camus also includes attempts to explain what the narrator calls the xenophobia of the settlers:

> Unemployment…was the most feared ill [by the *pieds-noirs*]. This explained that the workers, who in daily life were always the most tolerant of men, were always xenophobes when it came to work, accusing in succession Italians, Spaniards, Jews, Arabs and finally the whole world of stealing their work—a disconcerting attitude certainly for intellectuals who theorize on the working class, but yet quite human and very excusable.

Camus does not challenge the racism of *pieds-noirs* in French Algeria but instead justifies it. He uses class concerns (unemployment) as an explanation for the xenophobic reaction of the settlers. Through the narrator, racism occurs here as part of human nature, as an understandable reaction from ultimately likeable characters. Here Camus also uses his modest origins like a weapon, at times inferring that these origins give him an awareness and an authenticity lacking in some of his other interlocutors with more privileged backgrounds. This is yet another allusion to Sartre.

Perhaps oddly, the main adversary in this defence of French Algeria is not the Arab rebel, but the French anti-colonial left. In another telling passage, a settler who owns a vineyard is uprooting the vines in his property to ensure that Arabs will not be able to profit from them once they take back their land. When asked what he is doing by Cormery, the settler responds with what is meant to be bitter irony: 'Young man, since what we have done is a crime, we should erase it.'

Camus depicts the landowner as a tragic figure: an admirable hard-working man, an old *pied-noir*, one of those who 'are being insulted in Paris'. Yet this destruction of the vineyards harks back to one of the most sombre hours of the French conquest of Algeria: in 1840 when Alexis de Tocqueville's friends, General de La Moricière and future governor-general of Algeria Bugeaud, agreed to make the systematic destruction of Arab crops a policy to 'prevent the Arabs from enjoying the fruits of their fields'. This uprooting of olive trees and the destruction or confiscation of fields was a crucial moment in France's conquest of Algeria. Forced to leave that conquered territory, the French once again destroy cultivated land, but this time Camus describes them as being victims of an injustice.

This final unfinished novel, *The First Man*, becomes a platform for the expression of the white settlers' resentment. In particular, resentment against the metropole (the central Parisian authority but also mainland France in general) is present throughout, for example, in this exchange between the main character—Camus's

alter ego, Cormery—and a *pied-noir* farmer who tells him: 'I have
sent my family to Algiers [for safety] and I will die here. They don't
understand that in Paris.' The farmer's hatred of the metropole is
such that he expresses more respect for the Arabs who violently
oppose his rule. The farm owner advises his Arab workers to join
the Algerian resistance because 'there are no men in France'—that
is, the *pieds-noirs* will lose because of the weakness of the
metropolitan French. This is the despair of the white settler; he
feels abandoned by Paris and as a consequence resigned to
the rise of the Algerian resistance.

Another leitmotif in this work is the idealization of a time period
that pre-dates human existence. For Camus sees himself, through
Cormery, as torn between two universes, Europe and Algeria,
separated by the Mediterranean:

> The Mediterranean delineated two universes with me, one where in
> measured spaces memories and names were preserved, and the
> other where the wind and the sand erased the traces of men over
> great spaces.

That is, Algeria is the place with no memories, no traces of men.
Here Camus equates once more the notion of anonymity with
Algeria (and therefore with Algerians) but also on a moral scale
equates it with a place where human history is insignificant—which
allows the negation not only of the past of indigenous people,
but also of the recent past of colonialism.

The book's title is also an appeal to a past of a different kind. The
biblical connotations are evident, and it is interesting that Camus
thought about naming the first character Adam. This is part of a
*pieds-noirs* or colonialist fantasy that is unexpressed but present:
the notion that no man was present on this land before him—much
like Adam and Eve. This is a world vision that places European
settlers and European myth respectively at the centre of all things.
For example, Camus describes the main character as being born

'on a land with no ancestors and no memory…where old age found none of the succor from melancholy which it receives in civilized countries…'

In quintessential Camusian fashion, Cormery conceives of himself as being part of nature in a long stream of consciousness, which was to be the end of the novel:

> Like a solitary wave, always moving whose destiny is to break once and forever, a pure passion to live facing total death, [he] felt for life, youth, beings escape him without being able to do anything for them and abandoned only to this blind hope that this obscure force which for so many years had lifted him above days, nourished him immeasurably, equal to the direst of circumstances, would furnish him as well, and from the same tireless generosity from which she had given him his reasons to live, some reasons to age and die with revolt.

This 'obscure force' is Camus's thought—with all its strengths and limitations; the force is at once a refusal of intelligence and a regression towards nature: he is part of a greater whole, a wave in the sea. This unity with nature had previously helped Camus to transcend and escape the colonial realities. This is no longer possible; we are left with Camus's moving plea that this force come to the rescue, even in defeat. His realization is that the dream of a return to 'the good old days' is illusory; his colonial fantasy of the French as 'indigenous to Algeria' is dismantled. Camus's dismay is overwhelming.

The dream of a world ruled by nature rather than by society was shattered as well in his very first published novel. Returning to *The Stranger* we can see that the Arab was killed not only because he occupied the privileged space of Meursault's communion with the sea and the sun, but because he announced the inevitability of the rise of the Arab 'other'. *The First Man* reflects both an inchoate desire to negate this new reality (the coming of Algerian

**7. Victory celebrations in Algiers at the end of the Algerian War of independence.**

independence) (see Figure 7) and a long mourning of the old colonial order.

Throughout this final work, Camus was torn between his reformist, socially conscious leanings and his contradictory desire for Algeria to remain forever tethered to France. The text accordingly tries to legitimize France's colonization of Algeria in the most interesting of ways. Instead of attempting to speak to France's civilizing mission (a classic argument employed by France for centuries), or the need for colonization to maintain France's status as a great power (a more naked Realpolitik perspective which Camus employed at times), Camus describes the *pieds-noirs* settlers as revolutionaries. This new argument, which he developed in *The First Man*, was going to be the final attempt to resolve this contradiction for him.

Camus writes that the early settlers of Algeria had been a part of the French revolution of 1848; specifically he states they had been victims of the anti-revolutionary repression that took place in

June of that year and left for Algeria as a result. However, historians challenge the notion that there was a revolutionary French working class in Algeria. According to the leading authority on the matter, historian Charles-André Julien (1891–1991), the French workers who left France for Algeria in the aftermath of the repression of June 1848 became oppressors themselves: 'the workers and artisans who had survived the days of June 48 ... were those who were the most ruthless against Arabs.'

Camus tried here to claim the revolutionary struggles of 1848 to legitimize the presence of French settlers in Algeria. This view is unusual for Camus, who typically rejects human history as a frame of reference. However, for the cause of the *pieds-noirs*, Camus was ready to undo everything, even his own beliefs and ahistorical principles.

*The First Man* is an ode and a defence to the *pieds-noirs*. It is a tragic work where Camus for the first time faces his contradiction and resolutely chooses the side of French Algeria, as he wrote in his diary in May 1958:

> My job is to write my books and to fight when the freedom of my family and my people is threatened. Nothing else.

The emblematic expression of Camus's choice of his roots over justice was also his *cri du cœur* during a press conference in Stockholm on the occasion of his winning the Nobel Prize for Literature. When attacked by a militant of the FLN for espousing the cause of Eastern Europeans but not Algerians, he retorted: 'I believe in Justice, but I will defend my mother before Justice.' It was an odd response, because it implicitly recognized that the French colonial system was unjust. Put another way, Camus's response was a defence of his mother but also the admission that the cause of the FLN was just. Camus was broken on a personal level by the events in Algeria, as he wrote in his diary: '...Algeria obsesses me. Too late, too late ... My land lost, I will be worth nothing.'

Camus could not conceive of Algerian independence, nor could he conceive of himself as separate from French Algeria. It was his 'red line in the sand', the boundary which should not be crossed, the ultimate taboo. Algeria was the jewel in France's colonial empire, so important that the French authorities considered it a region of France. It was not just a military conquest; it was an administrative one as well. Camus was defined by colonial Algeria and could not live without it. Yet the paradox is that for many observers and readers, what remains is the sense that Camus persuasively uses the rhetoric of humanism while supporting French sovereignty over Algeria. This contradiction tore Camus apart while he was alive, but the illusion that he had resolved it remains.

Yet on some level Camus did resolve it. In 1956, with Algerian independence now a very real possibility, he put forth a more ambitious proposal for compromise. He wanted to give Algerians quasi-complete autonomy with a bicameral system. There would be two parliaments, one for Algerians, one for French settlers, and power would be shared equally except for two domains—the military and economic, which would remain the purview of the French. The result would have delegated day-to-day administration to the Algerians. Although Camus underestimated the balance of power between the French and Algerian sides, what he proposed for Algeria was a compromise similar in many ways to the current situation of many former French African colonies, which, though sovereign, share a currency controlled by Paris, and are the locus for substantial French economic interests as well as French military bases. This parallel between Camus's proposition for Algeria and what has emerged in most French-speaking African countries today explains in part why he has become the intellectual legitimization for today's neo-colonial reality, and why so many present-day Western political and cultural figures claim him as one of their own.

# Chapter 7
# Camus's legacies

One day while having lunch in October of 1957, Camus found out that he had won the Nobel Prize for Literature. He was not yet 44 years old, the second youngest winner since Rudyard Kipling. His first reaction was that André Malraux, his role model and mentor, deserved it more than he did. The year 1957 was a time of intense stress for Camus, who wanted to stay out of the limelight when the war of Algerian independence was raging—and the prize put him right back into it. There were numerous articles in the press about the award. Many were positive, but there were also attacks from the communist press and other critics, including Camus's former friend and mentor Pascal Pia. Many commentators did indeed wonder why Malraux did not get the prize.

In Stockholm to accept the prize, Camus was fêted by the committee and the local dignitaries but, as we saw, was also challenged by an Algerian student during a question and answer session. Camus's famous response putting filial love above justice was interpreted as a condemnation of terrorism by the partisans of a French Algeria, and as a statement of defence of the colonial order by the partisans of Algerian independence. It created a huge uproar and became a worldwide controversy, which was the last thing Camus wanted.

Camus died only two years later in a car accident. He might have said that his death had no meaning, though it does offer a glimpse of his personal life. The crash occurred on the way from his countryside house, in Lourmarin in the south of France, to Paris. He had originally planned to travel by train with his wife and two children, but instead agreed to accompany his publisher Michel Gallimard, who died a few days later from his injuries, his wife Janine, and his daughter Anouchka, who both survived. Up until the crash, it had been a pleasant two-day trip, in Michel's new sports car, and included two stops at Michelin-starred restaurants.

Before leaving for Paris, Camus wrote many letters, including three to his current mistresses: Danish model Mette Ivers, whom he called 'Mi'; Catherine Sellers, who acted in one of his plays; and arguably the great love of his life, Maria Casarès. To each he announced a different arrival date. This aspect of Camus's life later gave rise to many publications, including a book-length account of his last days and a huge volume of his private correspondence with Casarès, published in 2017, which spans fifteen years and includes nearly 900 letters, notes, and telegrams. (Almost sixty years after his death, the latter became a best-seller in France.) Such was the importance of Casarès in Camus's life that Francine herself was quoted as expressing concern for her well-being on the day of his funeral.

On 4 June 1960 and in the following days, all that mattered was that Camus had died and this was a national tragedy. The French radio employees who were on strike at the time temporarily suspended their movement to allow for the announcement of the news. Television cameras, numerous reporters, and of course friends and family attended the funeral in Lourmarin. Across the Atlantic, the *New York Times* dedicated an article to his 'absurd death'.

The question of his legacy immediately arose. When the draft manuscript of *The First Man* was found in the wreckage of the crash, it was first secured by the authorities on order of Malraux, and then returned to the family. After long deliberations among close friends including the poet René Char, Jean Grenier, and the novelist Louis Guilloux, it was decided not to publish the book immediately, as they believed it could be politically inflammatory in the midst of the Algerian civil war.

At the time of his death, in part because of the Nobel Prize presentation and the confrontation about Algeria at the press conference that followed, Camus was famous but not popular or universally approved. Only after his death did he become not just a famous writer, but a cultural phenomenon. His popularity reached a new level beginning with the fall of the Soviet Union. His works have been translated into numerous languages and *The Stranger* is a mainstay in the curriculum of many high schools across the Western world. Several of his novels and short stories have been made into films, his plays are staged around the world, and there are graphic novel adaptations of his works as well as countless scholarly publications. Politicians of all stripes frequently quote Camus and scholars cite him to support a multitude of often contradictory positions. Camus's most famous novel, *The Stranger*, is the direct inspiration for a pop song, and an Algerian writer penned an entire novel as its sequel.

What is it about Camus's works that inspires so many to quote, discuss, and use them as inspiration for books, films, and songs?

## Claiming Camus

One possible answer for Camus's current popularity is that the abstract quality of Camus's thought makes it transferable. He speaks to an abstract awareness of nature and mortality but does not tell his readers what to do with this awareness. Nor do his writings subscribe to any particular belief system. Camus does not have a programme or an ideology, and perhaps that partly explains his popularity.

Of course, this abstract quality opens the door for attempts to 'claim' Camus but they also lead to plenty of misunderstandings. Following the publication of *The Rebel*, one of the more striking misreadings of Camus's work took place in the Arab world, where it was largely misinterpreted as Sartrean, a revolutionary manifesto on the side of decolonization forces. A well-respected Native American scholar, Vine Deloria, praised Camus's passages extolling nature over human history in *The Rebel*, although Camus favoured space (nature) over time (history) not because of a love of nature per se, but rather because he saw human history as leading inevitably to the liberation of indigenous people, and thus to the downfall of French Algeria. Certainly, Camus openly espoused many causes in his lifetime, but only on a case-by-case basis, which led to multiple and differing interpretations of these ephemeral commitments. Camus has been described as a humanist, an anarchist, an anti-communist, a social-democrat, a colonialist, even an anti-colonialist.

Yet today it is not only Camus's ideas and various commitments that make him prone to so many different interpretations, but also his considerable popularity. Camus is not being misunderstood so much as he is being claimed. Conservative ideologue Norman Podhoretz famously stated that Camus is 'worth claiming'. A testimony to the opportunities Camus's writing presents for those many eager to associate his name to their cause is the fact that he is claimed across the political spectrum: not only by mainstream political parties, but also by radical Arab intellectuals and French anarchists. Camus's longtime nemesis, the French Communist Party, prints a daily newspaper that often quotes him on its front page.

French politicians are, as one might expect, leaders in this practice: the head of the far-right National Front, Marine Le Pen, began a January 2015 Op-Ed in the *New York Times* by quoting Camus. Emmanuel Macron, the centrist French president, imitates Camus's figures of speech and a copy of the luxury edition of

Camus's complete works appears on Macron's official state portrait, displayed in every mayoral office in France. The speechwriter for former French President Nicolas Sarkozy often quoted Camus. In 2009, Sarkozy proposed that Camus's remains be transferred to the Pantheon, the resting place of the great men of the French Republic. A controversy ensued during which Camus's son Jean rejected the proposal, which prevented the transfer.

The political spectrum of those who claim Camus is indeed broad: French anarchists are particularly insistent on depicting Camus as one of theirs; for example, a compendium of articles by leaders of the French Anarchist Federation is titled *Écrits libertaires*, which in French refers to a strand of anarchism and includes short articles by Camus. The Iraqi poet Abd al-Wahhab al-Bayyati publicly praised Camus as a supporter of revolution. Meanwhile, US President George W. Bush let it be known that he read *The Stranger* during the summer of 2006 (in the middle of the Iraq War).

Thus, Western politicians present a simplified version of Camus which is the mirror opposite of the vision of Camus as a revolutionary put forth by Arab intellectuals and French anarchist groups in the 1950s and early 1960s. Camus serves as a useful stand-in for humanism that is long on grand declarations but short on details, because when Camus wrote about politics he was for the most part loath to stake out clear positions.

Camus refused to openly choose between the partisans of a French Algeria and the pro-independence FLN. His compromise position in part explains why he is popular with Western leaders, who have intervened militarily and economically in the affairs of former colonies while simultaneously invoking humanitarianism and democracy as a justification. Essentially, this is Camus's contradiction in a nutshell: for many, he is the incarnation of the resolution of an impossible synthesis between enlightenment and colonial oppression. This is also why he is such an important figure in the Western world: he is the idealized vision of France's—and by extension Europe's—colonial past and neo-colonial present.

Camus spells compromise, even though he himself ultimately could no longer hold the middle line. Eventually he took the side of colonialism, stating in an interview that the Algerian demand for independence was 'emotional' and coming out strongly against it. Those statements and writings are routinely ignored because they do not fit with the popular vision of Camus as a concerned humanist rising above political concerns and preoccupations. Yet this contradiction between humanism and colonialism was present in many of his works from his earliest days, with varying degrees of intensity.

## Camus the cultural icon

Camus is also claimed in the cultural realm. In popular culture—especially in television—having a character invoke Camus is a shorthand way to make the character, and by extension the show, seem educated. The quote itself is almost irrelevant; what matters is mentioning Camus's name.

In cinema, Camus's works have over the decades inspired film stars (Alain Delon, William Hurt, Viggo Mortensen, Marcello Mastroianni) to pay homage to the author. The main cinematographic interpretations have tended to treat his works as monuments frozen in time. Another example is the pop band The Cure, whose first hit single, titled 'Killing an Arab', was something of an anthem for segments of early 1980s European youth. However, although the song is a short summary of the central scene in *The Stranger*, it also reflects and amplifies the indifference to Arab life already implicit in the novel. The death of the Arab serves as a pretext, an event that leads to existential reflections important to Western audiences.

What is almost casually implied as obvious in both the song and the novel is that there are things of much greater import than the killing of an Arab. The outrage in the novel is not that Meursault killed an Arab, but rather that he was sentenced to death for not mourning his mother. The pop song brutally magnifies this outrage, and some in France did not at first believe that the song was about *The Stranger*, such was the denial of the central event in the novel. Eventually, the changing political landscape and the globalization of The Cure's success led the group to modify the lyrics and change the title to 'Kissing an Arab'. Ironically, this change echoes what many critics have tried to do with Camus's work as a whole: soften the rough edges for specific political or commercial purposes.

In the French Republic Camus is indeed a secular saint. He embodies its ideal; he was after all the modest son of a maid and a vineyard supervisor who died on the battlefield. With the help of the French state and its educational system, he became a famous writer and a Nobel Prize winner; these accomplishments themselves are an advertisement for the French educational system and the French Republic as a whole. Camus has become something of a sacred cow in France. To a certain extent, it is perceived that criticizing him is akin to criticizing France itself.

Criticism also amounts to 'killing the golden goose': in the publishing world Camus is the source of considerable revenue. He offers what few other French authors do: the ability to read stories in a colonial setting that conceal the oppression of indigenous people. Most 19th-century French writers either revel in colonialism or are anguished by it; Camus displays indifference to it in his two most famous novels, *The Stranger* and *The Plague*. He represses the colonial unconscious, and this repression explains much of his lasting appeal.

But Camus has inspired more than just homages or attempts at appropriation. In 2013, the Algerian journalist, novelist, and chronicler Kamel Daoud wrote *The Meursault Investigation*, a daring and original sequel to Camus's *The Stranger*. In terms of structure, Daoud's novel resembles *The Fall* more than *The Stranger*, as it is a long monologue disguised as a dialogue between two men. The main character, Haroun, is none other than the brother of the Arab man Meursault murdered. The novel begins by challenging the unilateral European vision in the original novel. We learn about the man killed by Meursault, who was named Moussa, and about the grief of Moussa's family, provoked not only by the event itself but by Camus's and French society's utter lack of interest in them and their side of the story. In turn we discover that Haroun himself killed a young white man seemingly at random—a crime for which he is arrested.

However, *The Meursault Investigation* is not a work of denunciation, for we soon realize that the book is also a homage to *The Stranger*. Indeed, many themes and passages of Daoud's novel are singularly Camusian. For example, Daoud challenges the one-party Algerian state in a passage in which Moussa, after being arrested, is harangued by an officer of the FLN who brandishes in front of him the new Algerian flag, just as the prosecutor did with a crucifix in front of Meursault in *The Stranger*. Both Daoud and Camus confront a set of cultural values associated with what they see as alienating regimes, be it the French Republic or the newly independent Algerian state. Daoud's novel is thus both a critique of Camus's colonial bias and a celebration of his ruthless critique of other aspects of French society.

Another example of a different kind of Camus renewal is *Yazgi* (which translates to *Fate*), the 2001 Turkish cinematic adaptation of *The Stranger* directed by Zeki Demirkubuz. In *Fate,* Meursault is called Musa. After he murders two men, Musa is accused, convicted, and eventually exonerated for another murder he did not commit. The movie is set in Turkey, at a geographical and cultural crossroads between Europe and the Middle East, an environment which frees the story from the weight of colonialism.

In this setting, where race is a non-factor, Musa's indifference is perhaps even more devastating. Demirkubuz transforms into art the deep social alienation produced by a world ruled by family values, work, and the fatherland, just as Camus did in *The Stranger* with Christian values, office life, and social climbing.

## Camus lives on

Perhaps what makes Camus an extraordinary writer, one whose works millions across continents were and are able to relate to and identify with, is paradoxically his modest background. Unlike the majority of acclaimed French novelists, Camus came from a very poor family; before he became famous, money and how to earn enough to live comfortably were a constant source of worry. Camus as a young man always had a job. He worked when in secondary school; he worked when a student at university—in various unglamorous jobs doing mundane repetitive tasks at a desk in an office. *The Stranger*, Camus's most famous work, reflects this background. Camus heralded a new kind of hero in French fiction: the office worker, and a realistic one at that; his story was not one of social climbing.

Camus's greatest talent—his ability to translate a new set of rules, a new social reality, and a new way of life into art—is best illustrated by his notion of *bonheur*. In 1936, after the election of the left-wing coalition known as the Popular Front and the strikes and factory occupations that ensued, French workers won guaranteed vacations and a shorter working week. People started going on trips, mainly on their bicycles, and a whole new set of interactions with nature took place. With a shorter working week, people went to the beach, to the mountains, to the countryside. This was a national discovery and a sea change in the vast majority of French people's daily lives that goes on to this day. Nature became a source of happiness and an escape from the vagaries of life.

Only a few months later, given these changes, Camus first conceived of his notion of *bonheur*, a special relationship with nature, moments (never too long, he specified) of privileged interaction with the sun and the beach, as a source of happiness and a way to give meaning to an otherwise meaningless existence. Crucially Camus's concept and experience of the absurd heighten the significance of *bonheur* and as such they are inseparable. Camus's *bonheur* is the weekend, the trip to the beach, or the hike through nature. We might take these for granted today, but they were very much an electrifying novelty in the 1930s.

Moreover, Camus captured this new way of life like no other. His great and distinctive talent was to be able to transpose a new social reality of the world around him into his works with *bonheur*. His conception of nature, as a crucial and precious source of sustenance in an otherwise hostile world, resonates intensely with readers because it corresponds to how many live their lives now. Camus is an extraordinary writer because he was able to capture the daily, ordinary moments of his readers' lives (which were his own as well) and transform them into art. But he was also caught between colony and metropolis and his works at the same time reflect his colonial upbringing with all the shortcomings this entails, notably with respect to the lack of meaningful Algerian characters in his novels and plays.

This tension between generosity and indifference powers his works and recognizing it is an indispensable tool to assess his oeuvre. This tension has also made him the literary embodiment of the contemporary cultural and political contradictions of Western powers, an enlightenment at once oppressive and liberating, idolized by some and attacked by others. Camus is the writer of our global times.

# Timeline

| | |
|---|---|
| **7 November 1913** | Birth of Albert Camus in Mondovi (French Algeria). |
| **1914–18** | First World War. |
| **1914** | Death of Camus's father from wounds received at the Battle of the Marne. |
| **1924–31** | Attends secondary school in Algiers on a scholarship. |
| **1930** | Celebrations of the centennial of France's occupation of Algeria. |
| | First attack of tuberculosis. |
| **1931** | Meets professor and mentor Jean Grenier. |
| **1932** | Pursues studies at university in Algiers. |
| **1934** | Marriage to Simone Hié. They would split up two years later; divorce finalized in 1940. |
| **1935** | Joins the Communist Party. |
| **1936–9** | Spanish Civil War. |
| **1936** | Gets involved in theatre as a director and actor. Co-authors the play *Revolt in Asturias*. Finishes his master's thesis on Plotinus. |
| **1937** | Publication of *Betwixt and Between* in Algiers. |
| | Leaves the Communist Party. |
| **1939–45** | Second World War. |

| 1939 | Publishes series of articles titled 'The Misery of Kabylia'. |
|------|-------------------------------------------------------------|
| 1940 | Pascal Pia and Camus's newspaper suspended by French authorities. |
|      | Returns to France to work for Parisian newspaper. |
|      | Marries his second wife, Francine Faure. |
| 1942 | Publication of *The Stranger* and *The Myth of Sisyphus* in occupied Paris. |
|      | Camus is recovering from TB in the mountains of France. Separated from his wife Francine who is still in Algiers. |
| 1943 | Joins the French resistance at the end of the year. |
| 1944–7 | Editorialist for *Combat*, France's main resistance newspaper. |
| 1944 | Publication of his play *Caligula*. |
|      | Meets lover and famous actress Maria Casarès on D-Day. |
| 1945 | Massacres of Algerians in the towns of Sétif and Guelma on VE Day. |
|      | Condemns the bombings of Hiroshima and Nagasaki. |
|      | Birth of his twin children, Catherine and Jean. |
| 1947 | Publication of *The Plague*. |
| 1949 | Performance of his play *The Just Assassins*. |
| 1951 | Publication of *The Rebel*. |
| 1952 | Break with Jean-Paul Sartre. |
| 1954–62 | Algerian War of Independence. |
| 1956 | Camus proposes a 'civil truce' which is rejected by all parties to the Algerian conflict. Vows to no longer publicly intervene during this war. |
|      | Publication of *The Fall*. |
|      | Publicly condemns Soviet intervention in Hungary. |
| 1957 | Publication of *The Exile and Kingdom*. |
|      | Awarded the Nobel Prize for Literature. |
| 1958 | Publication of his articles on Algeria, 'Algerian Chronicles'. |

Albert Camus

| 1960 | Dies in a car accident with his publisher Michel Gallimard. |
| 1994 | Posthumous publication of *The First Man*. |
| 2009 | Proposal to transfer Camus's remains to the Pantheon. |
| 2017 | Publication of his personal correspondence with Maria Casarès. |

# References

*All translations are my own*

## Chapter 1: Camus, son of France in Algeria

Ch.-Robert Ageron, *Histoire de l'Algérie contemporaine* (Paris: Presses Universitaires de France, 1994) 62–3

Baudelaire, *Œuvres complètes I* (Paris: Gallimard, 1992)

Albert Camus, *Œuvres complètes I* (Paris: Gallimard, 2006) 44

Albert Camus, Jean Grenier, *Correspondance 1932–1960* (Paris: Gallimard, 1981)

Alexis de Tocqueville, 'Travail sur L'Algérie', 1841. *Œuvres I* (Paris: Gallimard, 1991) 704, 706

Charles-André Julien, *Histoire de l'Algérie contemporaine, tome I* (Paris: Presses Universitaires de France, 1979)

Herbert Lottman, *Albert Camus a Biography* (New York: Doubleday, 1979)

Lacheraf Mostefa, *L'Algérie: Nation et société* (Alger: Ed. Casbah, 2004)

Olivier Todd, *Albert Camus, une vie* (Paris: Gallimard, 1996)

## Chapter 2: Camus, from reporter to editorialist

Boussetta Allouche, *Albert Camus n'a pas compris les Kabyles* (Paris: L'Harmattan, 2017)

Albert Camus, *Œuvres complètes I* (Paris: Gallimard, 2006) 575, 585, 646, 656

Albert Camus, *Œuvres complètes II* (Paris: Gallimard, 2006) 9–25, 618

Albert Camus, *Œuvres complètes IV* (Paris: Gallimard, 2008) 351

Alice Kaplan, *Looking for The Stranger* (Chicago: U of Chicago Press, 2016)

## Chapter 3: Camus and the absurd

Albert Camus, *Œuvres complètes I* (Paris: Gallimard, 2006) 106, 228–9, 233, 257–59, 283

Albert Camus, *Œuvres complètes III* (Paris: Gallimard, 2008) 824, 1010

Albert Camus, Francis Ponge, *Correspondance 1941–1957* (Paris: Gallimard, 2013)

Alice Kaplan, *Looking for The Stranger* (Chicago: U of Chicago Press, 2016)

Conor Cruise O'Brien, *Camus* (London: Faber, 2015)

Edward Said, 'Camus and the French Imperial Experience' in *Culture and Imperialism* (New York: Vintage, 1993)

Jean-Paul Sartre, *Œuvres romanesques* (Paris: Gallimard, 1981)

## Chapter 4: Rebel without a cause

Ian Birchall, 'The Labourism of Sisyphus', *Journal of European Studies*, Vol. 20, No. 2 (1990), 135–65

Albert Camus, *Œuvres complètes II* (Paris: Gallimard, 2006) 437, 453, 1010

Albert Camus, *Œuvres complètes III* (Paris: Gallimard, 2008) 660, 1008, 1177, 1243

## Chapter 5: Camus and Sartre—the breaks that made them inseparable

Ronald Aronson, *Camus & Sartre* (Chicago: U of Chicago Press, 2004)

Simone de Beauvoir, *La Force des choses I* (Paris, Gallimard, 1972) 151, 158, 264, 354

Albert Camus, *Œuvres complètes I* (Paris: Gallimard, 2006)

Albert Camus, *Œuvres complètes III* (Paris: Gallimard, 2008) 412–30

Jean Grenier, *Albert Camus, souvenirs* (Paris: Gallimard, 1968)

Agnes Poirier, *Left Bank* (New York: Holt, 2018)

Jean-Paul Sartre, *Situations I* (Paris: Gallimard, 2010) 126–46

Jean-Paul Sartre, *Situations IV* (Paris: Gallimard, 2010) 90–129
Jean-Paul Sartre, *Situations VIII* (Paris: Gallimard, 2010) 375–412


## Chapter 6: Camus and Algeria

Ch.-Robert Ageron, *Histoire de l'Algérie contemporaine* (Paris: Presses
    Universitaires de France, 1994)
Albert Camus, *Œuvres complètes II* (Paris: Gallimard, 2008) 1010
Albert Camus, *Œuvres complètes IV* (Paris: Gallimard, 2008) 751–915
Charles-André Julien, *Histoire de l'Algérie contemporaine, tome I*
    (Paris: Presses Universitaires de France, 1979)
Charles Poncet, *Camus et l'impossible trêve civile* (Paris: Gallimard,
    2015)


## Chapter 7: Camus's legacies

Albert Camus, *Écrits libertaires (1948–1960)* (Paris: Indigènes
    Éditions, 2013)
Vine Deloria Jr, *God is Red* (New York: Putnam, 1973)
Yoav Di-Capua, *No Exit* (Chicago: U of Chicago Press, 2018)
John Dickerson, 'Stranger and Stranger: Why is George Bush reading
    Camus?' *Slate* (14 August 2006).< slate.com/news-and-
    politics/2006/08/why-is-george-bush-reading-camus.html>
Henri Guaino, *Camus au Panthéon* (Paris: Plon, 2013)
Norman Podhoretz, 'Camus and his Critics', *New Criterion* (November
    1982)
Marine Le Pen, 'To Call this Threat by its Name', *New York Times*
    (18 January 2015)
Kamel Daoud, *Meursault, contre-enquête* (Paris: Actes Sud, 2014)
*Yazgi* (Fate), Filmed and directed by Zeki Demirkubuz. Performances
    by Serdar Orçin, Zeynep Tokus, Engin Günaydin. Produced by
    Turkishfilmchannel, 2001.

# Further reading

A testimony to his ongoing popularity, there is a multitude of books on Camus; I have been deliberately selective.

## Biographies

There are two major biographies of Camus. The first is Herbert Lottman's thorough volume, which was viewed as slightly irreverent when it came out in 1979: it was only translated into French in 1985 (*Albert Camus: A Biography* (Corte Madera: Gingko Press, 1997)). There is also Olivier Todd's enormous free-flowing portrait, which ideally should be read in French; the English version has been edited and is much shorter than the original (in French: *Albert Camus, une vie* (Paris: Gallimard, 1997); in English: *Albert Camus, A Life* (New York: Carroll & Graf, 2000)). Other portraits include Edward J. Hughes's *Albert Camus* (London: Reaktion Books, 2015) and Robert Zaretsky's *Albert Camus: Elements of a Life* (Ithaca, NY: Cornell University Press, 2010), both laudatory. For a more critical perspective, see Patrick McCarthy's *Camus: A Critical Study of his Life and Works* (London: Hamish Hamilton, 1982).

## Studies on particular aspects of Camus's work or life

Ronald Aronson, *Camus & Sartre: The Story of a Friendship and the Quarrel that Ended it* (Chicago: U of Chicago Press, 2004). The best book-length study on the famous break.

Alice Kaplan, *Looking for The Stranger* (Chicago: U of Chicago Press, 2016). The biography of Camus's best-known novel, from the real life crime that may have inspired it to Kamel Daoud's novel. Superbly written and researched.

Agnès Poirier, *Left Bank* (New York: Holt, 2018). A fine introduction to what literary life was like in Paris between 1940 and 1950, through the portrait of many artists, including Camus. An original overview of his complicated relationship with Simone de Beauvoir.

Conor Cruise O'Brien, *Camus* (London: Faber & Faber, 2015). Originally published in 1970, Conor Cruise O'Brien's hard-hitting, irreverent interpretation of Camus's major works is still significant.

Edward Said, 'Camus and the French Imperial Experience' in *Culture and Imperialism* (New York: Knopf, 1993). The original critical post-colonial perspective.

# Index

For the benefit of digital users, indexed terms that span two pages (e.g., 52–53) may, on occasion, appear on only one of those pages.

Index

# CRITICAL THEORY
## A Very Short Introduction
### Stephen Eric Bronner

In its essence, Critical Theory is Western Marxist thought with the emphasis moved from the liberation of the working class to broader issues of individual agency. Critical Theory emerged in the 1920s from the work of the Frankfurt School, the circle of German-Jewish academics who sought to diagnose--and, if at all possible, cure--the ills of society, particularly fascism and capitalism.  In this book, Stephen Eric Bronner provides sketches of famous and less famous representatives of the critical tradition (such as George Lukács and Ernst Bloch, Theodor Adorno and Walter Benjamin, Herbert Marcuse and Jurgen Habermas) as well as many of its seminal texts and empirical investigations.

www.oup.com/vsi

# EXISTENTIALISM
## A Very Short Introduction
Thomas Flynn

Existentialism was one of the leading philosophical movements of the twentieth century. Focusing on its seven leading figures, Sartre, Nietzsche, Heidegger, Kierkegaard, de Beauvoir, Merleau-Ponty and Camus, this *Very Short Introduction* provides a clear account of the key themes of the movement which emphasized individuality, free will, and personal responsibility in the modern world. Drawing in the movement's varied relationships with the arts, humanism, and politics, this book clarifies the philosophy and original meaning of 'existentialism' - which has tended to be obscured by misappropriation. Placing it in its historical context, Thomas Flynn also highlights how existentialism is still relevant to us today.